MIND

BENDING

BELIEFS

Publisher: Independent Publishing Network.

Publication date: 11.11.2021

ISBN: 978-1-80068-155-6

Author: Anthony Augustine PhD

Email: info@anthonyaugustine.co.uk

Address: 671 Eccles new Road, Manchester, M50 1AY, UK

Website: www.anthonyaugustine.co.uk

Please direct all enquiries to the Author.

ISBN **978-1-80068-115-6**

Printed in country: UK

MIND BENDING BELIEFS

UNDERSTANDING SPIRITUALITY USING
PSYCHOLOGY, SCIENCE AND METAPHYSICS

WE NO LONGER NEED HOPE, FAITH OR
SUPERSTITION TO MANIFEST AS CO-CREATORS.

DEDICATION

We all have times when we experience a crisis of confidence, at the beginning of an uncomfortable inner exploration, or when standing on the precipice of change. Remember that you are loved, and you are not alone.

If you're examining different ways to view life, you will be challenged by your old beliefs as they clash with new ideas. I encourage you to stay strong in your quest. This conflict can be intense and that is normal. Like a butterfly transforms from the edge of a leaf, you too can spread your wings and take flight. With every stroke of your wings against the adversity of life, know that you will grow in wisdom if you embrace it. And as you remember who you truly are, you will evolve into an even greater version of yourself.

Connect to your inner strength and trust. Use honesty, courage and integrity as your moral compass, guiding you towards your destination. These virtues are sorely needed by humanity, now more than ever before.

To my children,

Meira and Kane, may you both live a life of inspired action, passion and, above all, manifest love, abundance and fulfilment as you align with your soul purpose. It's a joy to observe you both grow as your potential shines and radiates out into the world around you.

Always in my heart and mind,

Your loving father.

Confusion is the first step to knowledge
PS. The glossary is on the back

DON'T BELIEVE EVERYTHING YOU THINK

Manifesting desires and defining spiritual practice are important skills to be learned. This doesn't require hope, faith or Biblical terms of surrender that suggest there is no control over our destiny. Consciousness has distinct rules that, once learned, will supercharge all manifestations, reducing delivery time. Receiving prosperity, in every sense of the word, is part of a spiritual practice.

The landscape of your mind is a powerful force. Unfortunately, our precious attention is like a pack of horses; untrained and likely to lead in a direction that doesn't serve our best interests. Is it time to tame the pack? Once harnessed, the mind's capabilities, combined with the fundamental laws of consciousness, will open up a world of vast potential and countless opportunities.

Anthony Augustine inadvertently used the powers of manifestation all his life, moving through many industries, before shaking off his socially conditioned façade to engage with a life of authenticity and purpose. After nearly two decades of spiritual practice, he perfected his natural skills by mastering metaphysical philosophy combining the tremendous powers of the subconscious mind.

Augustine is a certified Subconscious Realignment Practitioner, award-winning trainer, mentor and coach to celebrities, professional athletes, movie producers, CEOs of global conglomerates and to European Royalty. Augustine holds a master's degree and PhD in the science of metaphysics, specialising in conscious-centred living. Augustine's Doctor of Philosophy was awarded by the University of Sedona, approved and regulated by the Washington DC department of education.

A medical doctor is focused on preventing death. A philosophical doctor motivates a life lived with prosperity.

American Metaphysical Doctors Association Member

CONTENTS

Introduction

The first half of Mind Bending Beliefs investigates beliefs from a psychological perspective. In contrast, the second half goes beyond the physical, bridging mysterious and esoteric knowledge, with new scientific evidence that offers a fresh explanation on consciousness and the Oneness.

When compiling my master's thesis and PhD dissertation into this book, I had to decide on the best order to structure the information. After much deliberation, I chose an order that would be the most accessible for every reader. First, questioning one's beliefs and how they're formed, which will open your mind to the evidence presented in the second half of this book.

One of the most important aspects to remember when reading this book, is to play with the facts before judging them from an old understanding. It is new thoughts and ideas that progress our intellect and empowers our intuition. If you choose to dismiss these new ideas, please ask yourself, is that because it's easier to keep on believing what you have always known? If so, consider that you might be dismissing new evidence because it conflicts with an older version of yourself, that may need updating. It begs the question: Is this way of life serving you? Or is it holding you back?

For example, broccoli, gram for gram has more vitamin C than an orange. Once a piece of information has been widely circulated and repeated, it is easy for us to simply accept it as fact. Crucially, if there's no further investigation into such collective knowledge and beliefs, then we remain on the surface of our reality. Hence, when a vitamin C deficiency is discussed, one would automatically believe that oranges are the solution, not broccoli.

Thankfully, science is now demonstrating functions of consciousness, and bridging the gap between quantum physics and ancient wisdom. The term, the Oneness, has been described in metaphysics and philosophy for thousands of years. That is to say, that we're all connected and live in a sea of energy known as the quantum field. What was once considered by mainstream science as 'the unknown', is now academically explained in science, biology, hydrology, epigenetics, and neurology.

We are all governed by moral and social laws that guide our behaviour. However, it's metaphysical laws that offer the key to prosperous living, which shall be demonstrated later in this book. Researching quantum physics has given me profound clarity on how our thoughts directly impact our reality. I continued to study a range of academic fields, to confirm this same hypothesis. Fundamentally, we are living in a sea of consciousness, and we can choose to either ignore or use its functions to our advantage.

The coming chapters will demonstrate how beliefs are intrinsic to the fabric of society and personal growth, by examining beliefs from a variety of academic fields, psychology, psychiatry, and philosophy. Exploring the deeper aspects of beliefs, presents an insight into human behaviour, cognitive capabilities, neuroplasticity, and more. Many beliefs are synonymous with religion; but, beliefs also shape every part of our reality.

Areas in life where what we believe had a substantial effect on our reality, range from our relationships, previous experiences, emotional wellbeing, education, personal development, spirituality, emotional stability, finances, careers, physical health, life purpose - to name a few.

This is because the fundamental aspects of life are wholly centred around what we believe. Whether that's a belief about others, our capabilities, or what we perceive to be achievable in life. Each one of us has a unique set of traits and talents, and to find our greatest gift to share with the world, is deeply dependent on what we believe is possible. For many, happiness is the only goal. Moments of happiness are often looked for in what's happening around us, in our social lives, holidays, sports, and meaningful milestones like weddings, child birth, and promotions.

Take parenting, for instance. Most caring parents aim to do what is best for their children. In reality, many parents focus on earning potential and stability as a way to happiness. Parents who have struggled financially in the past might concentrate on this area of life, and prioritise wealth over a children's natural abilities. Homelife influences both our conscious and unconscious mind. The belief that money creates happiness is conditioned into many as a child.

An empty void can form as a result of living through the lives of others, which can be examined over time with free will. It's a space that's not insidious or damaging, but a reminder to fill that space with a genuine desire. Often, we're rewarded with financial blessings after that void is filled, and the contentment that comes with it is a payment of its own.

Hugh Jackman, famous actor and performer, was once told by his brother, "*Dancing is for sissies*," which changed Jackman's own beliefs about the performing arts. Fortunately, his brother apologised years later and encouraged Jackman to follow his true passion. After signing up for lessons, Jackman went on to win an *Antoinette Perry Award* for *Excellence in Broadway Theatre*.

When young people are influenced by external voices and pressures, it can cause inner conflict, and a decision to pursue occupations that don't suit their authentic selves. Later in life, many of us notice a void between our occupation and sense of contentment, leaving us to feel like something is missing.

Introducing Beliefs

Do all survivors of child abuse grow up to be abusers? Do all children in low-income families grow up to be poor? These are sweeping generalisations.

Although poverty is often mistaken for a situation, its root cause is also a state of mind.

A mindset is constructed depending on how conscious we are of our thoughts. This process creates our internal representation of the world, which is unique to each of us.

Hypothetically, if a hundred people had the same experience simultaneously, each person would process the experience differently, creating their own set of beliefs, and use older beliefs to build on their own unique version of the world that is known to them.

Another example might be of a woman who believes that all men are misogynist, because growing up she witnessed her mother in a string of unhealthy relationships, which was then cemented as a child and adopted as a core belief into adulthood. This type of conditioning may repeat itself, even when the woman matures and enters a healthy relationship of her own. This is because a part of her internal reality is searching for alignment, based on the woman's conditioned expressions of the world.

The question is, are our subconscious beliefs aligned with our existence? If not, does the subconscious act out and encourage the environment to align itself with its version of the world? This example is to show how the formation of our core beliefs as a child could create a self-fulfilling prophecy, if one only observes dysfunctional or perhaps even abusive relationships.

Core beliefs are constructed in the early years of a child's life. Invisible to them, but their lives will be scattered with negative or positive after-effects. Growing up in school or at home, we're not taught to be aware of our inner world. It can feel like a guessing game for many, leaving us all at the mercy of our environment and the reactions of those around us. For any conscious act to be sustained, like a new habit, the mind requires both divisions to participate, conscious and subconscious. The manifestation of old habits and beliefs can go largely unnoticed when the conscious mind is unaware of them.

What we believe to be true exists only in our reality. We hold a subjective view of the world, and we're constantly at the mercy of who we deem an authority in our lives. Not just those who are close to us, but people in positions of power in which we place our trust. The ability to imagine or aspire, is also a conscious act. People talk about progress and growth in their life, but are rarely moved to action. What is the driving force, that separates those who do and those who don't step out of their comfort zone? Is that also down to what they believe?

Now I have widened your gaze into the ramifications of beliefs; we can go deeper into how, when, and why beliefs are critical to our lives.

What's more, we'll explore how to change our beliefs in order to live an inspired life, full of purpose, completely aligned with our authentic self.

Utilise the Oneness to Boost Your Client Success Rates

U nlike traditional therapy, counselling, psychiatry or psychology, when a client books a private session, they generally have two objectives in mind. Firstly, getting maximum results in the fastest time, and doing so whilst spending the least amount of money. With this understanding, I designed an exercise to review each session I offered, to perfect my skills and examine ways to achieve faster results. I attribute my progress with clients to several areas. In particular, an understanding of the power of the subconscious mind, conveying such knowledge effectively to empower clients, and by using techniques to communicate with the subconscious mind.

Here is a statistic that might bend your mind slightly:

95% of your life is attributed to your subconscious, while in comparison, your conscious mind is extremely limited in its abilities.

According to Dr Bruce Lipton, the conscious mind can receive only 40 nerve impulses per second, while the subconscious is more like a supercomputer, processing up to 40 million nerve impulses per second. This dramatically puts the ratio of capability into perspective.

"The (self-) conscious mind is the thinking you; it is the creative mind that expresses free will. It's the equivalent of a 40-bit processor in that it can handle the input from about 40 nerves per second." - Dr Bruce Lipton

The conscious mind is limited to between five and nine thoughts at any moment in time. For instance, can you listen to someone talk and read simultaneously? It's not possible. You might read a section of this book subconsciously and, by projecting your thoughts into the future or past, realise that you didn't comprehend anything of what you were reading. We all do that from time to time. The conscious mind has a fraction of the capability of the subconscious mind. While in comparison, your subconscious mind is doing millions of things simultaneously.

A facilitator is a blanket word for everyone that helps others. Whether that be alternative and traditional therapy, energy therapy such as reiki, Emotional Freedom Technique (EFT), or acupuncture. If you offer help to someone, their subconscious mind plays its role regardless of what modality you're using. The subconscious functions are vast and all encompassing, including beliefs, standards, values, habits, and primal instincts.

At this point in the book, let's just take a moment to marvel at the astounding functions of the body.

Do you consciously adjust the iris to manage the light that enters your eyes? Of course not. Imagine how much time that would take each day! The subconscious mind controls each organ and your body's homeostasis, which regulates your temperature, glucose, blood pressure, toxins, and pH levels.

You do not regulate your heart rate or breathing on a conscious level. If you decide to start running, your body knows the precise amount of adrenaline required. Your body automatically reduces blood circulation from the digestive tract, increasing blood flow to the arms and legs for immediate action. We take all of this for granted, because every day the body looks after itself as it's preprogrammed to adapt to new situations.

When one sits in front of a client or patient, our subconscious mind makes judgements faster than can be processed. The mind is evaluating posture, micro-expressions, responses to questions, tone of voice and probably hundreds of other variables simultaneously. It would be hard to keep track of each one separately - can you imagine? Fortunately, there is just one technique that aligns all of those subconscious reactions.

Once we learn how to intentionally step into the Oneness, we go beyond just holding space for our clients and experience a high vibrating state that transcends shame, blame, and criticism. We're talking about a frequency that guides, embraces, and provides for both facilitator and client. A space that allows us to surrender, and be guided by our clients' resources', because they have the answers! They have the ability, the fortitude, to hold onto pain. Imagine the power in that. What a fight to contend with, or perhaps a better question is: Why even try?

Once clients have been encouraged into this space, immediate change is possible, and not two to three sessions, just one! That's how powerful we all are, and that's how I get excellent results with my clients, by combining the quantum field with the power of their subconscious mind and their free will.

I'm a firm believer that our clients are our greatest teachers, once our chosen speciality is perfected. Those teachings have led me to conclude that beliefs are a significant aspect of one's personal development. Over the past fifteen years, I've drawn a firm line between those who are open to personal development and those with mental health issues that require longer, traditional treatments.

One of the apparent differences between these two types of individuals is what they believe. The belief that an individual can change, is a deciding factor for personal growth before a facilitator can nurture a client's desired outcome. The other significant influence is the presence of free will, from a conscious, stable, fully autonomous being.

On many occasions, I've been confronted with clients who, on the surface, demonstrated pathological tendencies that may require treatment from a psychiatrist, psychologist, or counsellor. However, upon further investigation, they did fall into the above parameters, but demonstrated a strong belief and stable mind to enable safe, immediate change, resulting in accomplishing their desired outcome.

When refining the spectrum of clients further, those who have good mental health can also demonstrate a defeatist attitude, restricting progress to the limits of their imagination. Each client has their own story, and how tight their grip is on that narrative is relative to that experience, as well as their ability to digest and attain a positive conclusion.

Subsequently, individuals will likely reflect on a positive experience with new beliefs and knowledge, when their conscious and subconscious are aligned. I have also observed this level of progress in clients who have suffered extreme trauma.

Observing each client as an individual, along with their attitude towards their proclivities, enables a swift identification of which clients can make an instant change, and which are using their symptoms for secondary gain. By referencing an individual's belief system, it's possible to ascertain if that belief is attached to their identity, and subsequently gauge how it serves them.

A commonality amongst individuals is the need for happiness, or emotional or physical pain relief. Happiness is an 'inside job'; It is subjective and indicates a unique journey for each person. However, the outcome is the same: A feeling of relief, delight, or joy, often leading to a brief harmonisation of our inner and outer world. How we get to this feeling depends on our resources, values, and beliefs.

The belief that an individual can be content is hinged on two variables: How conscious we are of our inner and outer reality, and what beliefs we hold in regards to happiness, including our definition of happiness.

In this physical world, we're conditioned to receive happiness from what we buy or participate in. This connects our happiness, or the absence of it, to our external world. If this influence stops, what happens when we no longer have what was making us happy?

Furthermore, if we get used to this cause of happiness and then the honeymoon period wears off, how will that make us feel? And how would we prevent it from happening? Is it possible, that a person must first understand what happiness means to them, before we go in search of it? Is the absence of this knowledge the same as not knowing our destination before we begin the journey? Or rushing the journey, because the destination seems more important?

Teaching the Oneness

When reflecting on my years of teaching, I have seen a trend. Most of what I have taught over the years falls into one of two categories: Knowledge to support techniques, or the practitioner's cognitive thought process, which highlights how our thoughts alone, can influence a session.

The latter is the challenging part of teaching because the objective is to shift the student's belief system, in order to comprehend how our intentions, thoughts and feelings are powerful enough to influence a client's outcome.

As a seasoned alternative therapist, many parts of my daily practice are second nature. It wasn't until the practice of teaching that forced me to take a fresh look at how I've progressed over the years, including why the techniques I use have helped clients and their successes.

When I started teaching subconscious realignment, I thoroughly questioned all of my knowledge, as I wanted my students to get the same level of success that I experienced. After reviewing each technique to understand its nuances, I wrapped up each one suitably in all my professional mistakes. Presenting the material in this fashion, with vivid explanations, supports students' learning process, because people love to learn through stories. This also enables me to appear more human, and my level of practice more achievable to students. By sharing the list of mistakes I've made, means that my students don't have to learn the long way around, as I did.

I teach with vulnerability in every class and explain what I got wrong, in the hope that they may be wise to these potential downfalls in the future. Consequently, this unorthodox style has been received well, and maybe a little therapeutic too. The main goal was and is to give the students a jumpstart in their career. For them to hit the road running, as it were.

Each class contained a diverse mix of students, naturally separated by their personalities. Based in Bangkok, people fly in from all over the world to train, and the most significant difference is how analytical or creative they were. I have found that the left-brained analytical types, struggle with what I would call, the 'Oneness', or quantum physics, called the quantum field.

This is understandable, as consciousness is an abstract subject. Intuition is also the opposite of intellect, and as Osho states, we limit our knowledge when we only perceive our reality intellectually. When it came to retaining information and systems, naturally, the intuitive ones struggled at first, so I knew who needed the extra care depending on their tendencies.

In the beginning, the focus in class was teaching the techniques well enough, so they felt confident in their practice. What happened over time was not expected and certainly not planned. I started to drop hints about the Oneness and its functions, but surprisingly nobody questioned it. Maybe a part of me wanted to push the boundaries of their perception and bring a little magic into their lives. I would always connect to the Oneness in a class demonstration, and every so often, I'd tell the group what I saw when the participant was in an altered state of awareness. Afterwards, I would casually ask the participant if I saw the same objects or colours to confirm what I observed in their mind. I wasn't keen to teach this skill as I wasn't sure if the whole group would expand their intellect to the unknowable.

One of the critical components to teaching is keeping a healthy flow in a group, all at the same level of comprehension.

Group dynamics can be a tricky task when there is a vast range of beliefs systems. As it happens, only the ones who understood what I saw acknowledged my "irregular insights," and I presume the more analytical ones chose to delete that information from their minds; I know this because they categorically never asked how my insights were possible.

Connecting to the Oneness is a skill I took for granted, and the more I taught subconscious realignment, the more I realised it's not a common practice. So, I adapted the lessons, found scientific ways to explain the Oneness and its functions, and brought the class together through group demonstrations on energy. Each class was becoming a combination of metaphysics and psychotherapy organically. It was even more exciting to teach, as I could now totally unleash my knowledge without restrictions or worrying if the functions of consciousness would be accepted, as science was successfully bridging the gap between metaphysics and psychotherapy.

When I completed my masters in metaphysics, the knowledge left me with a special assessment of consciousness and beliefs, which motivated me to write this book.

From teaching, I understand the staggeringly different ways people digest information. It was a pleasure to comprise enough information to explain consciousness and its functions for analytical and intuitive types.

After researching quantum physics and combining knowledge from other highly regarded doctors and scientists, the evidence of consciousness and its functions is undoubtedly academic. Furthermore, I acknowledged how imperative a practitioner's beliefs and attitudes are in manufacturing a successful session.

When I reviewed the eighteen principles, I designed to help practitioners in their practice, half of them were regarding metaphysical philosophies and the state of mind and not only applicable to the field of study I was teaching but universal for all modalities. Meaning any facilitator can apply these basic principles and see magnificent results. Why is that, you ask? Because metaphysical philosophy is universal to all. And beliefs are the most underrated manifestations of the mind, yet the most profound.

Imagine you and a client are sat opposite each other, your client has a symptom, and you have the skills to bring balance back to their life; however, they don't believe in you or your ability, and you don't believe they can be helped to recover. We could take this further and say you don't believe in your skills, and your client doesn't believe in themselves; now we have a problem. Picture that situation and ask yourself, how successful is your session going to be?

Although that situation would be rare, at least one would certainly hope so! It's not without verified degrees; ultimately, beliefs are the make or break of any successful session after the technique is perfected. The influence of beliefs also transfers to other modalities like acupuncture and different non-verbal types of therapy; if an acupuncture practitioner is in a place of non-belief, how does that affect the meridians?

Interestingly, it's only complementary and alternative therapy such as reiki, acupuncture, homoeopathy, etc., that use the word energy. However, the mind is proven to be an energy and separate from the brain which means all modalities are working with energy. The law of thermodynamics states, energy cannot be created or destroyed but changes from one form to another. Ask yourself this, how are you influencing the energy of your mind or that of others?

Now I've given a quick preview of what you can expect, let me unpack this paradigm-busting knowledge and empower you to be the best version of yourself possible. For one simple reason, the greater you become, the more you work on yourself; comprehending those shifts within your clients will become easier. Once you believe you can make fast, safe and effective changes in your life, it is easier with your clients, and holding that space for change will happen with more grace. Unless they are sabotaging that experience, but that's a different topic.

Fast Phobia Cure Done at an Airport Boarding Gate

I love spontaneous moments, a session in a coffee shop or airport; the environment is irrelevant when you and your client are as one and their desire to change transcends any previous needs.

When my father died, I was working several contracts in Asia, so I took the first flight back to the UK. On arriving at the airport, I took the opportunity to get some work done before the gate opened. I've never been one to queue and enjoy waiting until the last moment to board.

On this occasion, I was sat across from an older gentleman. I glanced up on a few occasions and noticed he also was waiting to board last. Our eyes connected, so I took the opportunity to say hello and ask if I could inquire why he was waiting. He replied, "I'm not looking forward to getting on the plane." I could see by his physiology; it was a lot more than a casual discomfort, and he was downplaying how he felt. He sparked my curiosity, and after asking him why he looked uncomfortable, he informed me about an extremely turbulent flight some thirty years ago; and since then always has trouble flying.

My instinct was to put my laptop down on the seat next to me and go a little deeper into his history. I have no restraints when helping others; I don't need a significant chair or equipment; my work tools are subjective. What I've found to be essential are free will, intent, and beliefs. Using these, I've witnessed many thousands of clients make fast, safe and lasting change.

As a seasoned facilitator of change within others, I knew my ability to help this gentleman was only the start. What I required from him was his intent to let go of this phobia; for all I knew, it could be a secondary gain. Meaning, on a subconscious level, he was using the phobia to receive from others in the form of attention. He could have been using the flight to sabotage the arrival at his destination. None of that went through my mind because I had two short questions to qualify his level of intent; with each answer, I was automatically preparing to do a session with him. My last question was this: If you want to let go of that, you can close your eyes. He immediately closed his eyes, and I knew he was ready to let go.

To be clear, he was sat across an aisle in a terminal at one of the biggest airports in the world, Bangkok airport, and 90% of the passengers had already boarded. Still, it was too late, I was now in a session, and the fact he closed his eyes told me he was ready to let go; that's all the commitment I needed. He could have asked me why or said, don't be silly, and carried on reading his paper, but he trusted. On reflection, the need to let go of his phobia must have been so strong that trusting a total stranger was the better option. Or perhaps it was a combination of my confidence in asking him to close his eyes or the feeling of certainty I gave off? That's indeed a feasible contribution, but I'm sure this event was already planned on a higher level of awareness.

I stood up and walked across the aisle where he was sat with his eyes closed. I immediately suggested he went deeper into an altered state of awareness and guided him into a metaphor to work through his phobia. Once the metaphor started, I was no longer in control of the situation, how long it would take or how successful it would be was now the responsibility of his conscious and subconscious mind. I didn't take that into account before I asked him to close his eyes; it was more of a knee-jerk reaction.

I've never experienced a situation like that, so I was flying by the seat of my pants. Excuse the pun!

We were about ten minutes into the session, and the speakers sounded our names. At that moment, I was unwavering in my present state to support him. There was zero doubt that he would end his torment from carrying this phobia; my belief in his ability was absolute. The metaphor was over, and I checked to see how he felt. The response was one of relief. He took a deep breath and, on the exhale, it was as if I saw thirty years of flying stress release from his body in one breath, and then his body slumped into relaxation mode.

I knew there was now alignment within him. As I looked up, two stewards were standing next to us. I put my fingers against my lips to suggest they stay quiet and held up my hand to indicate I needed five more minutes. They frantically nodded their heads with crossed lips. I looked around, and the gate was empty. All the passengers were on the plane.

I turned to the gentlemen and asked him how powerful that feeling was, the feeling that had been with him for so long. He assured me it was extremely powerful. I asked, "Is it possible to ask that powerful part to now help you feel secure when flying?" He replied, "Yes," and as he did that, I noticed his posture change again. His head raised, and his shoulder set back in a confident state.

At that moment, I checked in with my intuition to see if I had time to complete the session the way I know best, which is to surrender entirely to the client and their journey. I disregarded all the surrounding pressure and spoke the words that gave total responsibility to him at that moment, the ultimate deciding factor, so he knew to the depths of his soul if he had finally let go of that phobia. I spoke the words, and I knew that I'd done my best, and it's up to him. I said the magic sentence, sat back in my chair and waited.

The sentence was a bind to the action of opening his eyes. I took a chance because his subconscious reaction could mean the session wasn't over, but I was quietly confident because I saw how his body reacted to the metaphor throughout the session. Now that could have been a pretty mess to be in if his eyes didn't open, as time wasn't on our side. That also would have meant there was more work to conclude before the realignment was complete. I trusted in my intuition, took a deep breath, and stayed focused in supporting his process, regardless of the now five stewards eyeballing me from different parts of the boarding gate.

I can only imagine what they were thinking. Their reactions were a combination of amazement, bewilderment, and confusion! Not knowing what I was doing or what the result was going to be. Also, in the past, clients have always taken their time. The main reason for that is they are in an altered state, so time is altered. It's super-fast. Half an hour in the outer world can seem like ten minutes in a client's inner world.

I think my heart did skip a beat at that point because my logical mind kicked in, and I didn't want to miss the flight. When he opened his eyes, we all sighed with relief and smiled at each other. I had no idea what these stewards were thinking, and they didn't have time to ask. I inquired how he felt; he said, "great." I told him, "We need to rush as everyone has boarded."

I believe in the law of reciprocity, not because I want to receive, but because life rewards us when we need it most if we do our best. I didn't book extra legroom in my panic booking to get back to the UK, and at 6' 2," my flight could have been very uncomfortable. As we entered the aeroplane, I noticed this gentleman was about to sit at the bulkhead next to the emergency exit with good legroom. The steward asked me if I wanted to sit next to him during the flight. I smiled and gracefully received my small blessing. I don't take a running tally, but it did cross my mind the Universe was working through that stewardess.

Before the flight took off, this guy was in a deep sleep for over four hours. It's an eleven-hour flight to the UK, and I was happy for the 'me time'. When he woke, he told me it'd been thirty years since he slept on a plane and how relieved he felt.

Unfortunately, I don't remember his name, probably because it was an everyday event for me. What I do remember was the story of his daughter and how she needed help and enquiring about therapy. He told me that now he understands how powerful the mind is, he will support his daughter's choices.

If you were to ask me what part of that experience had created a lasting impression, it was the butterfly effect from my life to his daughter's. I remember how deep in thought he was about his daughter when he spoke of her.

This guy had a moment of comprehension that I knew would change how he would support his daughter and her needs. He ironically looked like my father, who had just passed and a familiar stoic nature and similar age. Knowing what era he was from gave me an idea of the emotional distance between them and how better prepared he will be next time he sees his daughter, which gave me a warm kismet feeling.

Unlike the other anecdotes in this book, I have written testimonies; maybe one day through this book, this gentleman will get in touch and share his progress because once you let go of one monumentalised phobia, that opens the floodgates to all other possibilities.

I wonder how learning to communicate with your client's subconscious mind could help them with their progress?

The Powers of the Subconscious Mind and Influenced Beliefs

Before fully comprehending the belief system, we must first understand some functions of the subconscious mind that influences how beliefs are created and act like a filter navigating our lives. The subconscious is constantly watching for repetition and consistency. Once this simple directive is fully comprehended, we can evolve our character and personality. Otherwise, it's left to chance, hope, or superstition.

There are two ways a belief is formed, a learned behaviour or a significant event.

The other deciding factor is you; the same boiling water hardens an egg but softens a potato. Essentially, it's your personality, character, and genetic make-up that influence an outcome, accompanied by the fluid circumstances of reality and its extremes.

The subconscious mind functions constantly observing for repetition, and consistency means continuous sensing and monitoring trends in your environment. The subconscious mind isn't troubled by inconsistent tasks. Otherwise, it would be making programmes that have no use. Programmes are created to free up necessary bandwidth in our limited conscious mind.

There are approximately twenty prime directives of the subconscious, with millions of subcategories encompassing the functions that help us process reality. To comprehend how beliefs are formed, we will cover eight functions:

1. The subconscious mind stores all memories

2. The subconscious mind influences perception
3. The subconscious mind makes new habits
4. The subconscious mind utilises repetition or significant events to adapt
5. The subconscious runs and preserves the body
6. The subconscious mind is the emotional mind
7. The subconscious mind is symbolic
8. The subconscious mind doesn't know the difference between right and wrong

First, using a significant event as an example:

If you think back to a friend or family member with a phobia. You might remember how restricted they were. It's easy to see the effects in daily life and no mistake about the inconvenience. Using the power of the subconscious mind accompanied with strong intent is the perfect combination to overcome a phobia.

I would go as far as to say a phobia is one of my favourite challenges to facilitate realignment because it's so apparent. Unless the phobias are used for secondary gain, and the individual is receiving compensation from its effects. That is a different type of client with multiple connecting challenges requiring the consultation to dig deeper than the phobia itself, past the symptoms to the cause. This type of client would fall into the parameters of a complex compulsive habit.

An excellent example of secondary gain is a friend of mine, Sunny; we would go for dinner on occasions. Generally, I would be the designated driver, and when arriving at his apartment I would sit in the car park waiting for extended amounts of time, often bordering on the rude. However, I knew his condition. He had a complex compulsive habit and proclivity to check light switches and sockets and do his hair repeatably before leaving his apartment. He was aware of my occupation, and on one occasion, I did a casual deep dive to find out the cause.

It transpired the catalyst to this behaviour was from a death in the family. While attending his grandfather's funeral, he made many trips to the toilet to wash his hands. The highly charged emotional event coupled with his actions to alleviate the tension started a habit he later would have no control over because it was an instant resource that worked at the time. The subconscious is the pragmatic mind. Once a powerful event is concluded, it will return to those beliefs leading to thoughts, feelings, and actions until updated.

Unfortunately, he was thirteen years old and had limited coping mechanisms and no awareness of how that significant event would influence his mind in later years. On one occasion, I mentioned to him as a passing comment, "You know I can help you with that, right?" His response was, "I like it," and with a smile, no less! That was the end of the discussion because I know where that compulsion resides, and both his conscious and subconscious mind must agree to be helped before lasting change can occur.

Sunny's subconscious mind believed those actions helped him; in fact, they probably do because in states of stress, it can seem, he is exhibiting a modicum of control. However, what he interprets as relief is more of a comfort blanket or welcomed distraction.

It's often tricky offering help to friends or family as they may have an opinion of you that may be outdated or don't understand or value your training. When something is free, it has zero value. Individuals must have a clear idea of what they wish to achieve, identify their pain, discomfort and know how their life will benefit once they put down what is no longer serving them. A thorough consultation is always required.

The Mysteries of Learned Behaviours & Significant Events

Next, we will discuss how learned behaviours can form beliefs. Cast your memory back to the first time you learned how to drive. You might remember who your instructor was, maybe your father, mother, or uncle? You can probably recall how nervous you felt. Wondering how you will pass your test because there are so many things to learn, right? All drivers start at the same place, and it doesn't last long for many and over a short period, as the brain is designed to, adapt, learn and adjust to new behaviours.

You may have been directed to a quiet neighbourhood to learn new manoeuvres during your driving lesson, such as turning corners. You are focused on the sequence of actions in those moments, braking, indicating, dropping your clutch, checking for other cars and pedestrians, and turning. Probably not in that order, but I am sure that your awareness is present, not thinking of what you are doing after your lesson or reminiscing about the previous day. There are only three options—the past, present, and future. When learning anything new, we are present, fully aware and apply our intentions to start the process of retaining information for new habits.

Some individuals have a natural dispensation to complicate the process with excess fears, self-doubt, or anxiety. For them, it's a little more complicated as they must overcome their limitations before learning. For this instance, assuming we are dealing with an individual who isn't suffering from cognitive restrictions. They will go through a process of learning to drive through repetition.

Back to your imagination, you are in that car you learned how to drive. Now, if we go three years into the future, it's been many years since you passed your test. You might even be driving around the very same corner you learned before you passed your test. Are you thinking about indicating? Checking your clutch or what gear you are in? No, because your subconscious mind observed the patterns and rules of driving and made it an automatic habit. Now, when you drive, you are free to project your mind back to the past or into the future as your subconscious mind is driving the car automatically.

Why is that? Because now you have more bandwidth for your limited conscious mind to think about the past or future when the subconscious mind is running the car in the present moment. Have you ever driven to the wrong destination by mistake or taken the wrong turn because you were in a state of wonder or deep deliberation? Your subconscious mind can, when required, make decisions on your behalf. Pretty cool, isn't it?

Are the powerful divisions of your mind starting to make you aware of how supportive and ironically how simultaneously limiting they can be?

The function of the mind observing repetition isn't just for manual tasks; the mind also watches for your thoughts and feelings. If we are not careful, we can create habits that we struggle to change in later years. The worst outcome is not being aware to observe the behaviours that we unknowingly programmed in the past. The subconscious mind is a double-edged sword as it doesn't know the difference between right and wrong, good or bad. You can create bad habits and beliefs just as quickly as good ones; this is free will.

When we are not living a life of purpose, on purpose, we are indeed living a life from habits, and if that continues long enough, cruising through life. We are not making new empowering choices but repeating what is preprogrammed by our self or society. If life is absent from conscious-centred living, we are essentially going around in circles repeating the same behaviour.

The caution from this function is straightforward. Be aware of what you think.

We assume no one knows what's going on in our heads, but that isn't true. We project our intentions physically and metaphysically, and both have significant consequences depending on the severity of our thoughts and the length of time we unknowingly conditioned ourselves.

Keeping a clear mind free from negativity, resentment, hate, self-pity, and such is paying our positive intentions forward as our present thoughts construct our future self. The subconscious mind is watching, and habits from harmful thinking form programmes that are limiting. You may not see the effects immediately, but in later years, harmful subconscious programmes with destructive beliefs about yourself or your environment could be running in the background and causing havoc in your life. Which you are not even aware of, much like your subconscious driving a car while you are consciously on autopilot—giving you the ability to think about the future or the past.

Beliefs are also programmed into us as children through the repetition and consistency of observation. Suppose we observe destructive behaviours as a child, and the repetition is great enough. In that case, deep-seated ideas of our reality can grow into actions and behaviours that may cause harmful outcomes later in life if that individual isn't conscious enough. There is a famous saying, "show me your friends, and I'll show you your future." Society is constantly conditioning, and those nearest play a significant role in that development, either from a positive, inspiring perspective or the alternative.

Occupation note

In Sunny's story, I deliberately avoided the clinical term *obsessive-compulsive disorder* (OCD). Due to the fact, my public liability insurance is specific to my training, and I'm not a traditional therapist or observed and regulated. However, I can deconstruct such terms and use techniques to identify the emotions connected to psychological terms and guide clients to let go of what no longer serves them; if they show the right degree of intent and comprehend their symptoms. That's within my remit, training and obligation as a facilitator. There is a fine line, and I would suggest using your experience to guide how close to that line you sail if you are an alternative therapist.

Childhood Beliefs and Adult Consequences

I f you have or know young children, you may have noticed how their tendencies, character, and expressions, both physically and mentally, can be like their parents or caregivers. Facial expressions, mannerisms, and vocabulary are all subject to an immediate influence.

These observations are created from their sensory interpretations, what they can see, feel, and hear. It's not until later in life that children's beliefs can mirror their parents in aspects of life. As most parents are not conscious about their own beliefs, they have no idea how they programme their children. This lack of self-awareness, in turn, passes on attributes from parents to children that may or may not be productive, depending on a child's consciousness and internal representation or innate skills to analyse events, as opposed to being at the mercy of them.

As I specialise in subconscious realignment, one effective technique I use is regression. On countless occasions, I regressed clients into their early years, often wondering how they remembered such events at two or three years old. I'm less impressed with the ability to recall memory since having children. Not that I marvel any less in the magnificence of the process but seeing how children develop opened my eyes as to how early they learn new skills and capabilities. From experience, many one and a half to two-year-olds can make their own decisions on preference and taste. There are no restrictions for a healthy toddler that's guided with love and has a wholesome environment to learn.

When using a regression technique, it may be unreasonable to generalise that all clients regress to their actual childhood. However, is that relevant if the adult makes the required progress? The subconscious has a powerful imagination, as seen in dreams. It could be constructing a metaphor to work through a challenge, like it does in the REM (rapid eye movement), the sleep cycle that processes and concludes events as we sleep.

I was aware of the two academic variables, but I wasn't confident in comprehending them until I met James, an investment banker. A simple regression technique I use called 'happy times' regressed James from forty-five-years back every five years as far as four. Some individuals are hard-wired to draw on pain, so the pre-talk includes only going back to happy, joyful times to ensure you are not triggering the client's negative memories. Also, checking the type of childhood the client has experienced is imperative, as a small portion of society tend to grow up in unloved families.

What fascinated me about James was his ability to regress every five years and tell me the events with the date, month, and year. His recollection was unfathomable and made a lasting impression with me as to the mind's abilities. Regressing thousands of clients gave me insights into how young children start to form beliefs.

Furthermore, I witnessed a trend of clients whose subconscious mind was going back to early years to resolve limitations. Previously I presumed they were metaphorical events; now, I understand beliefs are developing in our early years.

When conducting a consultation, I'm constantly surprised at clients' recollections of events connected to their beliefs.

Children experiencing significant events and learned behaviours at two years old and younger have fully functioning minds, with the ability to conclude their reality. Those conclusions can be subconsciously revisited for the rest of their lives while unaware of the cause and the event. Probably due to our long-term memory holding very few early memories accessible to the conscious mind. Nevertheless, the beliefs are certainly active regardless of the ability of memory recollection.

Childhood beliefs are deep within the psyche, and only the symptoms are observed; when questioning clients, they rarely remember when or how beliefs were developed. I would go as far as to say, only twenty percent are accurate in their recollection. Also, a strong deciding factor is the age of the child at the time of the event that caused the beliefs. I came to this conclusion as I asked clients before proceeding with all regressions to compare the results with their memory. This comparison has provided profound insights into the abilities of the mind and how beliefs are formed.

For instance, an MP came to see me one afternoon. We can call him Gerrard. Gerrard was employed by the British parliament for many years and visited me with a list of challenges he wanted to change. It must have been fifteen items long. On investigation, we worked through each item on the list and concluded that the items underpinned his lack of confidence and affected his promotions, which was his primary concern.

We investigated his childhood experiences, and he suggested his confidence was affected when he moved from one part of London to another and was without his childhood friends and support system. Gerrard was convinced his confidence started to diminish when he was twelve years old, and he recalled the event that was the catalyst to his lack of confidence.

Gerrard explained how moving made him feel insecure because his friends were more like a group who supported and protected each other. He had a good think about what event caused his lack of confidence and told me about an instance of walking down a street in London and being confronted by a gang. He felt intimidated as the gang singled him out.

Now we had a benchmark for my professional insights; we started the session. I regressed Gerrard back into his subconscious mind until it was ready to recall the actual event that happened.

Occupation note

Before using regression, I checked if there was any trauma in his childhood to ensure not to trigger or relive unwanted events. In my vast experience, only metaphors are required to disconnect the emotions from traumatic occasions. When I asked Gerrard, I watched if his reply was congruent with his body language, eye contact, vocal expression, intonation, and tone. A client once fooled me, and the result was not empowering. Now, I ask and make my assessments even after a client's confirmation of an absence of trauma and press further if required.

What transpired was a memory of being in class in his new school, the teacher was asking questions, and Gerrard was able to answer most of them. One afternoon, a group of boys from the class circled Gerrard in the playground, threatened him, and said, "If you don't stop making us look stupid by answering all the questions, we will hurt you." At that moment, Gerrard concluded a new belief that his intelligence can be dangerous and he should not be viewed as more intelligent than his peers.

While still in an altered state of awareness in the session, we did some inner child work, negotiating with his inner child to resolve these limiting beliefs that his knowledge could cause him physical harm. The inner child agreed to let go of those limiting beliefs, freeing Gerrard from his restrictive behaviours as an adult.

In defence of the younger version of himself, he did the best he could with twelve years of resources at hand. However, in his early fifties this younger version was still active and firing emotions into his consciousness, restricting progress in his professional life which subconsciously was the substitute for his school life. When guiding Gerrard back to full waking consciousness, he arrived with a new updated version, no longer restricted by an adolescent self.

Occupation note

Inner child work is a formidable technique and can cause further implications to clients if done incorrectly. Due to the severity of inner child work (if done improperly and beginners inevitably make mistakes), I only certify students after direct observation and instruction. Attempting to learn such techniques without direct supervision and revisions is highly irresponsible, including online training or ‹learning' from a book.

Working with client's beliefs in the right emotional place is the highlight of my career. However, I have been confronted with different individuals with the same symptoms but the outcome has varied. These types of clients have encouraged me to explore different techniques to increase success rates. Which led me to the 'five stages of awareness' that I designed as a simple system to identify what stage a client is at in their progress of letting go of their challenges.

Aristotle is one of the first recorded philosophers, and one of his famous quotes, regarding a child's development in the first seven years, is now supported by psychology. Aristotle's view is centred around how a child is conditioned effectively due to the absence of any other beliefs. By installing beliefs at an early age, a child then has a predisposition to search for consistent evidence as they manoeuvre through life, to substantiate what they already know to be accurate, building on those beliefs deep in their psyche.

"Give me a child until he is 7, and I will show you the man." - Aristotle

Denise Winn references Toch Hans, a social psychologist, and outlines the following. Conditioning by society and its dogmas has a drastic effect on children's belief systems and acts to restrict free-thinking outside of a modified reality. In addition, children may be guided to exhibit specific belief strategies to receive praise, approval, even love from parents in exchange.

These belief strategies can create a fracture within a child's aspirations, as their most natural inclinations towards endeavours are shrouded by their parents' desires, views of achievement, or unique ideas of success. Leading to the observation children are essentially indoctrinated by their parents or nearest caregiver because they are a blank canvas with no other beliefs to fall into conflict.

Winn explains how their environment reinforces these beliefs as children go to schools in the same area as they're raised, and that indigenous society shares similar beliefs. Winn explains how psychologists call this reinforcement, 'perception set', to absorb from our environment what we're set to receive, and unconsciously filter out what isn't relevant to us.

"The combined effect of childhood indoctrination and the socialisation process, at its most successful and effective level, serves to blinker an individual to reality and create a dependence on a belief system – any belief system."
- Winn

The Five Stages of Awareness

Analyse a Client's Level of Intent Using the 'Five Stages of Awareness'

Stage one - Unaware of destructive attitudes

An individual is unaware of their habits, attitude, or behaviour and undoubtedly a subconscious projection.

Stage two - Becomes the observer BUT in denial

Internal recognition is forming, but no responsibility for being the catalyst of negative events is accepted.

Stage three - Acceptance, repeat & apologise

An individual is conscious of their limiting actions, and accepts their behaviour. They move into a repetitive cycle of exhibiting their negative behaviour, observing it, and apologising.

Stage four - Searching for help

The conflict from the individual's conscious mind is great enough to search for help with their own free will.

Stage five - Commits to change

An individual is dedicated to finding a suitable modality and committed to change, and personal growth. Using the five stages, you can observe all behaviour falls into a category. Does the individual know who they have become or are they oblivious to their actions?

This system is suitable for all human interactions, in relationships at work and especially with clients. Giving you the ability to assess an individual's level of self-awareness and offer an idea of how long it may take to help them adjust their behaviour.

You cannot un-ring this bell; now you know this system, you can assert boundaries in your life according to your resources. Resources are unique to you as an individual; only you can assess how capable you are in assisting others without letting a situation affect your long-term state of mind. If you can manage an individual's behaviour and facilitate progress and self-discovery, you can adjust your boundaries according to the progress you observe.

If you are a traditional therapist, you are more likely to be presented with patients in the first stage who are referred to you by court order, doctor's referral and couples counselling, etc. Individuals in the first stage may have personality disorders who are oblivious of their conditioning but function in society and hide their inner world from the outer world sufficiently.

When individuals with personality disorders enter a romantic relationship, the superficial mask doesn't offer everyday protection from their dysfunctional self. Many internal challenges are displayed but isn't that one of the metaphysical points to a relationship? To be seen to the core, to stand naked and trust in the growing process together. This concept is only possible when both parties are aware enough to see themselves and acknowledge personal development as an essential part of relationships. Otherwise, one is growing without, and away from the other. You can lead a horse to water – but you cannot make it drink.

From a metaphysical perspective, there is no right or wrong, no coincidences. We are all perfect and living with a sense of amnesia of who we truly are. Each of us has a choice to wake up to our authentic self that comes from a place of love, compassion, acceptance and let go of our conditioning. Once we see who we have become, we can, if we choose understand those parts of ourselves without shame, blame or criticism. We can then start to heal faster, as acceptance of our previous self is liberating.

The Dark Side of Conditioning

Denise Winn discusses Edward Hunter's conclusions about the mind and the different ways we are conditioned to believe what is real about our reality. The most severe type of conditioning is brainwashing, which was coined in 1950 by a CIA employee and author Edward Hunter. The translation is from the Chinese word 'hsi-nao,' meaning 'to cleanse the mind.'

Hunter followed up on the Korean War by writing books on how the Chinese changed prisoners' beliefs to suit their political views to collaborate with communist China. The prisoners of war were victims of mind control techniques generally used to condition Chinese society to the rule of communism but later used to treat those caught during the war. The methods were so effective up to seventy percent of the 7,190 prisoners were successfully conditioned to believe in communism and signed petitions to end the war.

However, only a tiny percent of the ones that complied continued with the conditioning after the war.

"Authors, such as psychologist expert Joost Meerloo, are fearful of the effects of mass manipulation, cite that of 7,190 US prisoners held in China, 70 percent were swayed by Communist propaganda to make confessions or sign petitions calling for the end of the war – though few 'remained' Communist after the war and repatriation."

Winn continues to explain the correlation between knowledge and beliefs. While both are mutually exclusive, a firm knowledge of what you believe is essential to have a solid belief to withstand interrogation to break a belief. Knowledge creates self-confidence and a strong disposition to stay firm in one's own beliefs. The lack of knowledge, therefore, leaves individuals in a precarious position when confronting their beliefs.

"A belief is a belief because it isn't knowledge." - Denise Winn

The Amazing Correlation Between Knowledge and Beliefs

Beliefs are pre-set filters to build the perception of our reality. These internal commands or guiding codes for life are built from observations that can be limiting or empowering.

Using Gerrard as an example, Winn's insights confirm the conclusion, correlating the functions of beliefs and knowledge. Gerrard's idea of why his confidence was affected was an assumption. Although feeling intimidated by that gang was causing him to feel anxious about his safety, the gang's mindless actions didn't go beyond menacing Gerrard.

The combination of physical threats in the school playground and the coercion to suppress his knowledge caused a new belief. Reflecting on the consultation with Gerrard, he was unaware of why his confidence was hidden, but he had a long list of symptoms without knowing the cause. Breaking the belief that Gerrard had low confidence was simple, because there was no knowledge attached; his belief was forged via a significant event that threatened his safety.

'Conditioned Helplessness' or 'Learned Helplessness' Affects Mental Health

Beliefs also affect how we respond to life via our mental health, as Dr Seligman explains the theory 'conditioned helplessness,' ergo how conditioning affects an individual's internal representation of stressful events. Moreover, until society becomes aware of this unconscious conditioning, negative beliefs will remain a stimulus-response projected by the subconscious mind and accepted as 'normal' by individuals exhibiting such behaviour. Dr Seligman explains how we can condition our minds to be more optimistic than pessimistic and how that affects our mental and physical health.

Dr Seligman coined the phrase 'learned helplessness' and how this belief traps individuals in a cycle of accepting defeat because it's a previously effective strategy. He explains optimism and how 'explanatory style' is an internal skill that creates a conscious act of explaining why events happen. This explanatory style aims to reduce negative thinking by decreasing the destructive internal dialogue when circumstances are not favourable. Explanatory style moves an individual away from hopelessness and the pessimistic mindset. Furthermore, the way we internalise events reflects how helpless or energised a situation can influence individuals.

Dr Seligman expands on how personal control and conscious awareness of self are the keys to identifying which strategy is used, either learned helplessness or an explanatory style. If an individual has a pessimistic attitude, shining the torch of awareness can influence their attitudes and beliefs toward a greater optimistic view.

When it comes to taking responsibility for our personal development, Dr Seligman explains how to overcome learned helplessness. His consensus is that beliefs form pessimistic or optimistic views in life and conscious thinking combined with individual control is the key to optimal living. Dr Seligman outlines his strategy to overcome learned helplessness by using an optimistic explanatory style to interrupt a habitual pessimistic view supporting a negative belief system. He explains how many adverse events can be reframed to find a new conclusion that empowers and protects individuals from depression.

"Learned helplessness is the giving-up reaction, the quitting response that follows from the belief that whatever you do doesn't matter." - Dr Seligman

Psychological Labels
and Their Effects

We don't have to venture too far when searching for examples of how easily some individuals are influenced by those seemingly in a place of authority. The most recent image in my mind, in early 2020, was a lady on the news who stood over her sink emptying an entire case of the famous Corona beer down the drain! Similar thoughts among patrons had connected the established beer brand with the "new virus."

Now take a moment to comprehend the influence a doctor has over their patients. We have all blindly handed over our critical thinking skills or stopped questioning the opinions of others, professional or otherwise. But to what consequence? To make an informed decision, we must assess all new situations thoroughly. The fact I'm not licensed to diagnose or alter a regulated physician's prognosis works in my favour. Simply reviewing a client's history and offering insights into how the mind works leads many clients to new empowering conclusions.

Tom, not his real name, is a successful businessman living in Singapore. In his consultation, he informed me he was bipolar. I have been in the energy of bipolar individuals, and it didn't feel the same as the energy he transmitted; my intuition told me to go deeper.

Bipolar is a significant label, and I was intrigued to hear why he was recommended this prognosis. Fortunately, his memory was outstanding, and we went back to his early years as a boy and thoroughly discussed his youth, feelings, attitude, and internal representation of his world. We came to solid conclusions about his nature as a boy before moving forward to other areas of his life, from school to college and university.

There was a constant trend of an introverted child, and I explained the benefits of that personality type and the downside that can manifest if his inner and outer world are not correlating. To make a point, I brought Tom back to the present day, and we highlighted how his introverted nature was complimenting his life, and he added to the list confirming what he had taken for granted as an introvert.

What was a surprise was his negative view of introverts. His beliefs were absent of facts or a psychological description but a comparison of how he felt extroverts viewed an introvert. He didn't understand those personality types, and after providing a complete account of both, he could make an informed judgment. We then returned to the part of his life that his "bipolar" started, and he recalled a moment at university.

Tom was at a party watching a young man dancing on a pool table, being the heart and soul of the party and getting plenty of attention. This party, he informed me, was the first of many, and as Tom talked, I could see him reminiscing of those times. Tom elaborated into a realisation he had while watching his fellow student dancing on the pool table. Tom said, "I didn't want to be the shy, quiet type anymore," and as no one knew him, it was a fresh start to be whoever he wanted. Tom was smiling as if he had discovered a code in the matrix to change how others could see him. I was getting a very firm idea of how his behaviour confused his prognosis.

The consequence of his severe transformation added extreme lows in his life, having achieved a high energy extroverted lifestyle and succeeding in his desire to be well known at university. However, it wasn't sustainable. Tom informed me of a chart he made that followed his drastic shifts in energy levels and behaviours, and it followed a three-month cycle of ups and downs. We reviewed his natural tendencies; we cross-referenced them to his life and virtues. Finally, he compared what we discovered with his born inclinations.

There is a magical moment when you coach a client to their realisations, it's a tedious but rewarding technique, but the crumbs must be close enough together to join the dots. Tom was smart and followed each question and statement gathering the correct evidence as we went along his timeline, defining his authentic self. When we arrived back to his present day, I left a moment of silence.

It took a few minutes for Tom to get his senses back. He was in a bit of a daze as he reconstructed his life but now knowing who he was meant to be and how he had created this alter ego. The evidence was conclusive, and as we both sat there in silence, he had a few false starts, beginning a comment, pausing, and then answering his own questions. After a short while I could see he was resigned to the fact that his personality wasn't what he thought it was.

He was simulating the evidence. It was as if I could hear the cogs turning in his mind. I gave him some time, and when he looked ready, I asked, "What do you think?" He looked over and told me, "I'm not bipolar." I'm just an introvert trying to be an extrovert."

We had been in the session for nearly ninety minutes, but from the moment he presented me with that label, I knew from tuning into his quantum field with my intent he wasn't what he thought he was. I also knew I had to prove it. The whole session was orchestrated to shine the light on those three words that would ultimately free him from his old self construct.

We ended the session and made an appointment for a few days later, as I knew he wasn't out of the woods yet. The next step after that realisation was to align his new conscious version with his old subconscious self.

He asked me what he should do with the medication he was prescribed. I told him I was not licensed to answer that, but he could do what he feels necessary and inform his doctor as some chemicals are addictive, and weaning off may be required.

After realigning his reality with his conscious mind, the next step was to inform his subconscious mind to let go of what he had created, the habit and desire to be what he wasn't, his alter ego if you will. Without the conscious conclusion, the subconscious wouldn't know what to let go of or why and there would be no lesson to learn. Therefore, we have free will, to become aware and choose. The session was a success, and he went on to value his natural introverted nature and relaxed into life, drug-free, I might add.

The skill to observe personality types contributed to that successful session. However, the major work was done in the subconscious mind, where the habits are projected into his consciousness. Does that mean all bipolar labels are misdiagnosed? Certainly not. Unfortunately, the story highlights how reviewing a client's past from neutral ground can extrapolate essential information rather than being biased in prescribing medication.

If Tom was taught how to observe his thoughts in his early years, might that road trip down the adjacent life be prevented? Dr Seligman remarks how people must be mindful of the actions that encourage negative emotions within them. He highlights how "specific psychological doctrines" have stripped away such responsibility by renaming normal behaviour such as impolite, rude, or other negative behaviours as neurosis. He comments that when such individuals accept their new labels, it orchestrates further damage to an individual's life.

Labels may, in some instances, permit individuals to continue inappropriate behaviour by relinquishing responsibility for their actions instead of being accountable and owning the outcome of their choices, decisions, and actions.

Dr Seligman postulates if an individual changes their internal strategy regarding failure from internal to external, 'it's not my fault; It's bad luck.' That type of attitude affects one's level of personal responsibility to manage their emotions and direction. Dr Seligman explains one circumstance that shifts from internal to external is justified when one is depressed.

It seems depressed individuals take a considerable amount of responsibility for external events and more than is required. Dr Seligman also mentions that individuals must take responsibility for their behaviour to evolve their character and personality.

Using the past to evolve instead of assigning external excuses, we set an internal strategy that supports personal growth.

"I am unwilling to advocate any strategy that further erodes responsibility."
- Dr Seligman

Neuroplasticity and the Brain

When conducting a consultation, sensory acuity is critical to observe how empowered a client looks about overcoming their challenge to achieve their desired results. The mind is energy, the software to the hardware, the brain. If the software isn't convinced, the hardware makes no change. Empowering an individual on a conscious level is liberating, and when communicating to the subconscious mind, three parts are vital, imagination, concentration, and intention. A client's intent increases all three; the higher the intent, the greater the brain's chance to adapt. I've witnessed this in countless sessions, those who are not committed or emotionless even, make little change.

Those who are enthusiastic, excited even nervous demonstrate a strong desire to amend their behaviour. Those who have fast, dramatic shifts in sessions generally feel exhausted, discombobulated, or tired afterwards. From experience, this type of response typically indicates a successful session. If I had a penny for every time a client came back to full waking consciousness and expressed an intense physical reaction and later reported a dramatic change in their behaviour, I would be rich.

At the beginning of my practice, I was marginally concerned as no practitioner wants to witness clients feeling physically strained, especially when the work is therapeutic. Now I smile and inform clients that the radical shift in the brain's neuroplasticity creates that feeling, and it's a good response. Now I suggest that come the evening, they will have a deep sleep and feel fresh and revitalised the following day.

My educated guess is their brain has undergone a massive shift in neuroplasticity, habits, and beliefs instantaneously, causing a physical effect. Suppose I correlated the emotionless clients with low intent and no physical or emotional impact during and after the session. In those cases, they are the individuals that had the least benefits from an identical session.

A fundamental dichotomy that researchers of human cognition face are the mind-brain connection; very similar to the chicken and the egg theory, which came first? Moreover, which is the greater influence? Doctors Bender and Sidney explain how modern scientific research concludes that the brain is influenced by the mind and undergoes a process of structural change that rewires the brain, called neuroplasticity.

This structural change makes it possible, at will, to change how individuals behave and react to situations. In turn, creating the constant potential to evolve and adapt to our environment. Therefore, making a defeatist attitude a self-fulfilling prophecy, if you believe you can change, the brain is designed to adapt to your intent.

Neuroplasticity also supports free will as the brain's plasticity is not by chance but a direct result of the mind's intentions. In turn, by focusing on different activities, for example, meditation or the simple act of applying gratitude, an individual can restructure the brain's frontal lobes that influence cognitive skills like planning, organising, personal responses, and social behaviour, to name a few.

"New research and technology have reported that the living brain can continue to change with your thinking, and these discoveries are relevant to overcoming self-defeating beliefs and behaviours." - Bender and Sidney

The Dark Night of the Soul – Core Beliefs

The question is, are our clients held to ransom by their subconscious mind and its generalisations? Clients genuinely don't know what they are conditioned into until they observe their feelings, thoughts, and actions.

Society is not taught from childhood how to be the observer of self; it's not a known practice, and in adulthood seen as to be a harrowing experience, few refer to this as 'the dark night of the soul.' Shining a light on the darker part of oneself is an important and challenging process that can lead to a transition if the shedding of our previous self is complete.

The very thought of such awareness is frightening enough for most individuals. I live to wonder how much more progress society could make if what is referred to as the 'dark part' of our personalities or the obstructions within are illuminated and learned from.

Fortunately, the second time individuals take a closer inspection into themselves, and each time after that, the healing is faster, and the process provides more profound lessons. Crafting a unique personal development journey is an essential part of life as opposed to stumbling across our darker parts in horror. Or ignoring those darker parts and resigning to a life of blissful ignorance and letting evolution inevitably happen around us.

A man who views the world the same at fifty as he did at twenty has wasted thirty years of his life. – Muhammad Ali.

Bender and Sidney continue to explain how beliefs are not constrained by right or wrong and have a significant amount of influence over our behaviour, depending on how conscious we are of those beliefs.

When the subconscious blocks us from achieving a specific outcome or activity, this holds our choices at ransom. Beliefs also filter unconsciously, meaning we may bypass specific experiences because the subconscious mind has discretion on our behalf. However, in the past, any discretion was once a conscious act, whether deliberate or not, and continues to be observed by the subconscious mind.

As for core beliefs, Bender and Sidney explain they are instilled early on in an individual's life and is part of the base foundation. Since most core beliefs are created when we are young, the negative beliefs can be limiting because knowledge and wisdom are restricted; the internal representations are not based on a fully formed mind or understanding of life from an objective, fully autonomous perspective. Beliefs can vary in how constructive or restrictive they are, depending on the age they were formed.

"Beliefs are thoughts that influence what you think about yourself and the world you live in, and they can either be reasonable and logical, or unreasonable and illogical, and they may be positive or negative."
- Bender and Sidney

The Power of
Emotional Triggers

Managing clients' triggers is essential and a compassionate act. There is an antiquated idea that clients who suffer from trauma must discuss their experience to release the emotional charge. I've never found this to be necessary when helping clients with mild to severe trauma. Three stories from clients come to mind; the first client had a car accident and was trapped in the car for forty minutes until the emergency services could rescue her. During that time, she had to contend with the three other passengers in the car that died on impact.

The second was a sexual assault on a minor, and the third was a man who broke down when trying to explain his story. I can only assume by the level of physical anguish he was also sexually assaulted. I didn't have to find out as the session was a success without asking him to repeat and inadvertently relive that traumatic experience.

All sessions were successful, but the latter is relevant because he didn't need to share the trauma. I can count on one hand the number of times a male client has broken down in a session, but this was different. It was obvious he was feeling the need to protect himself. As his shoulders scrunched up and his head lowered, he could not give me eye contact as he tried to catch a breath and regulate his breathing. The physical reaction to verbally addressing his challenge shocked me. It happened suddenly. I was taken aback by how fast he went to that dark place once I asked him what he wanted to let go of.

Once I saw how severe his reaction was to my question, I changed my voice, projecting an even greater understanding and caring persona. I wanted to reassure him and keep my boundaries, as I wasn't sure if this was a control drama pulling me into his story. If that happened, the session would no longer be about progress but using the time to justify how he felt. I gently said Tod's name and told him in a smooth, nurturing voice, "It's okay, you don't have to tell me the details to let go of that feeling." I vividly remember how he looked at me, almost in disbelief, accompanied by a strong physical reaction as if he was relieved. He didn't have to rip a plaster off what was a sore wound. I waited for him to gain control.

As a practitioner, the emotional state of my clients is mainly in my hands; questions can either change a client's state of mind away from their pain or take them deeper into that place of anguish. The type of sessions I provide work effectively without going to such dark places.

This reminds me of a flight from Bangkok to Koh Samui late one evening. It was the last connecting flight from China where I was coaching one of the presenters for a national talent show, the Chinese equivalent of Americas got talent. I was also invited to meet Jackie Chan and one of China's famous singers Wei Wei, who incidentally has sold more records than Michael Jackson and Madonna combined. No doubt, the pure magnitude of the Chinese population was a contribution to that statistic.

On my connecting flight back to my home on Koh Samui, we travelled on a much smaller plane due to low passenger numbers from Bangkok. It was loud, cramped, and uncomfortable. The young lady next to me looked disturbed, so I started a conversation with her, and she told me she didn't like flying. I was exhausted from travelling from China. Still, I could see by her physiology; she was only marginally anxious but not uncontrollably. I knew a simple distraction would be suitable to help her, and not too much effort on my part, which was a relief.

I quickly noticed what type of clothes she was wearing, presumed she was a yogi and asked her about her first experience that got her into yoga. It didn't take long to induce the lady into her rich inner world. She smiled and, with much excitement, told me she was on her way to Koh Phangan, which is a smaller island beside Koh Samui, to do her teacher training and went on to explain her passion for yoga.

I was obvious with my eye contact to test if that made her feel comfortable, and fortunately, she locked on, so I knew she wouldn't be looking out the window behind me. I listened with enthusiasm, turning my posture in my seat to let her know I was fully engaged in her stories.

Next, I felt the plane take off while she was deep in her passionate conversation, and as the plane levelled out, she stopped and said, "Oh, we have taken off." I smiled, she sat back, and we both relaxed. If you get a chance to ignite someone's passion, it's a beautiful experience to observe if you can do that when someone needs it most; it's also an underrated but perfect distraction.

We digress, let's get back to Tod. After settling him down, I started empowering him with knowledge of the subconscious mind and its powers. I shared other stories of how fast previous clients let go of their trauma and how he could, too. With each story, I could see his posture lifting, and it wasn't long before he felt relaxed again and in control. I honestly didn't know where that session was going. It could have quickly turned into a counselling session if that was a greater need. I was also relieved when he started to relax. It's not comfortable watching another person cry, especially bordering on hysterically, but it's also highly unprofessional to comfort a client with anything other than your voice.

Any traditional therapist reading this is probably gasping in disagreement while shuffling around in their seats because other theories would suggest allowing Tod to express his emotions would be beneficial. If operating from a traditional therapy perspective that would be a standard protocol. However, the skills I developed, work in just one session, and Tod came for one session expecting a result. I'm not concerned with his triggers or compounding them; that's merely the symptom. I aimed to acquire a stable state of mind and work directly with the cause, the programme that reacts to his conscious cognition or a stimulus from his environment. To then utilise the power of that portion of the mind that programme resides, the subconscious mind.

The session was a success, and months later, he wrote to me explaining how much he had recovered. If I were a traditional therapist, I would have been inquiring why he reacted that way, followed by months of observation and assessment. The only requirement necessary for subconscious realignment enabling recovery is a healthy intent to disconnect those emotions from their memories. It's that simple. Once clients have worked on their traumas with specifically designed sets of metaphors, they can safely revisit the memory and take the learnings.

Applying the techniques to individuals at the right time in their recovery has a significant impact on the success of the sessions; this is an essential skill.

The environment stimulates beliefs; Bender explains how triggers evoke memories from our subconscious mind into our consciousness. The trigger is a stimulus from any of the senses with a strong connection to a significant event. If events are not substantial, the subconscious doesn't hold those memories in high regard and is less likely to have any triggers.

A trigger can be either positive or negative, which activates a memory projected from the subconscious mind. In addition, Bender breaks down the triggers into three different types:

Perturbations are negative emotions, elaters are positive, and harmonisers are empowering.

In order for the subconscious mind to quickly connect to an individual's consciousness, perturbations have the highest authority. They act as a warning system when danger is sensed, or an individual is required to protect themselves. Once the immediate threat has passed, the perturbation stops ensuring the stress hormones have ceased excreting. Protecting the body from an overload of stress hormones that can cause other symptoms if exacerbated.

"Triggers in energy, psychology can be considered forces that instantly link a present-day event to a memory and the associated feelings, whether or not you are aware of a connection." - Bender and Sidney

Food, Nutrition and its Influences on the Mind

The holistic view of personal development and wellbeing is essential. Once you learn one healing modality, adding a certification in nutrition that covers a little biology will complement your practice. Food can be used as medicine, and a lack of certain nutrients may lead to cognitive deviations of perception, leading to less than favourable choices and actions.

Stress triggers food choices high in sugar or fat that may influence an individual's hormone balance. Both excess fat and sugar increase the body's acidity and, if levels reach a critical mass, every system in the body: organ systems include the skeletal, muscular, lymphatic, respiratory, digestive, nervous, endocrine, cardiovascular, urinary, and reproductive systems may be affected.

Acidosis, along with inflammation, are two underlining causes of every illness and disease. Dr O. Young states, *"We are alkaline by design but acid by function."* From the twenty-seven years I have been casually studying nutrition, understanding food from a chemistry perspective has never failed me. There are many fads and fashionable diets. However, once you learn to regulate your body's pH balance, all the body systems will self-regulate to achieve homeostasis.

Although beliefs conditioned by our environment can affect our minds and bodies, both adversely and favourably, depending on our internal representation, food is also an influence in that internal process, as different nutrients affect our hormones. Food types have a direct association with how effectively we direct our consciousness to live a balanced life.

Hunger has multiple purposes from the subconscious mind. Hunger's quintessential purpose acts as a warning system that the body requires energy or hydration. On many occasions, these are confused, and overeating can be due to thirst. This concept is beginning to percolate down into society as common knowledge. However, there is a third misperception.

The subconscious mind cannot stick a flag out of your ear or send you a text message when it requires a specific nutrient. A diet devoid of micronutrients, vitamins (not artificial in a bottle), and minerals will encourage your subconscious mind to fire cravings into your conscious awareness. This can be confusing when feeling hungry shortly after eating. The subconscious assumes you will eat different foods than previously and get what the body requires to maintain health. Ponder this; you can be overweight and be malnourished; now there is a twentieth-century problem if I've ever heard one.

The mind's preferred type of communication is, once again, cravings. The same is said for ex-smokers who haven't told their subconscious mind they have stopped smoking. Leaving many ex-smokers to put weight on as the craving for smoking is confused with the same feeling of dehydration, hunger, a programmed scheduled eating time or lack of nutrition. So, next time you get a craving, interrupt that instinct and ask yourself a few questions to identify its purpose.

The first can be, are you eating for comfort or a nutritional function, the latter maintains health and wellbeing. In contrast, I don't discourage all comfort foods if there is a knowledge of the consequences. Not knowing why or what we are eating is the primal cause of disease and illness.

The difference between a healthy field of soil or a field of dirt is simply the microorganisms that comprise the ecosystem to sustain life – the little fellas. The same goes for our digestion; eating a balanced diet feeds our probiotics, producing the non-essential amino acids. That's why they are called non-essential. The essential amino acids the body cannot make. Therefore, we are required to eat these nutrients to maintain homeostasis, health, and well-being.

The same bacteria make eighty percent of the serotonin in our gut. Eating for pleasure one hundred percent of the time will categorically lead to illness and possible disease. If you are feeling down, ask yourself what percent of your diet is functional and for your health. If you are ill often, I can guarantee functional eating is not on your radar. Food for thought?

If you are feeling down regularly or struggle to focus, the chances are your gut bacteria, also known as the second brain, is struggling to maintain your health due to a lack of the prebiotic building blocks they require. The moral of this story is, look after the little guys, and they will look after you. Your gut bacteria have thousands of responsibilities, not just digesting your food, remember it's not just what you eat; it's what your body can absorb!

Depression linked to Inflammation

Serotonin is one of the 'happy hormones' the body produces. One of its tasks is to encourage the mind and body to feel good about successfully achieving tasks. Therefore, a positive internal representation of reality is not enough to sustain a balanced healthy mind. As a result, examining what we eat is a critical obligation for a healthy mind and body and maintaining conscious-centred living. Surprisingly eighty percent of serotonin is made in the digestive system, and a poor diet can affect levels excreted that encourage that underrated feeling of contentment.

Perlmutter explains how tryptophan, an amino acid found in some nuts, seeds, eggs, lentils, and some meats, is the precursor to serotonin. Serotonin positively affects our mood and lowers cortisol, which is triggered as a result of stress. However, when inflammatory chemicals (the result of stress hormones, illness or poor food choices) are present in the blood, tryptophan also converts into the kynurenine pathway.

The kynurenine pathway is observed in a direct correlation between inflammation and depression. Therefore, an individual's ability to remain optimistic about challenging events can be severely impaired due to a diet encouraging inflammation, acidosis and or a stressful lifestyle.

Perlmutter also suggests that the kynurenine pathway also reduces the prefrontal cortex's capacity and function, responsible for cognitive behaviour, personality expression, and decision making. Depression formed from a lack of self-awareness is also linked to abnormalities of the prefrontal cortex.

To conclude, eating food groups that encourage inflammation in the body prohibits our happy hormone precursors to convert into serotonin, making a positive attitude challenging to maintain. *"The increased activation of this kynurenine pathway has recently been implicated as a key link between inflammation and depression."* A whole-food, balanced diet is also essential to maintain a stable, positive mind.

Placebo, Mind Over Matter

What we believe to be true in this reality, is true. Clients decide to believe in your modality when they book a session, whichever segment of the healing industry you are in. When I first became a facilitator and chose a modality that I wished to specialise in, I was under the impression I was making the changes within my clients. It is an allusion created by our ego to inflate self-worth. The work is done by the client and is their choice. The good news is, once practitioners stop taking responsibility for a client's success, we can also stop taking responsibility for our client's postponement of success.

Although a considerable amount of conditioning goes into the complex compulsive smoking habit, one acupuncture session can stop a smoker successfully if they desire. Acupuncture demonstrates how an individual can overcome all psychological conditioning with pure will and intent, the placebo effect. However, if an individual is confused and questions the process, the outcome may be affected.

As all smoking habits are constructed with a robust set of beliefs, on many occasions deconstructing a smoker's belief system before they stop is required for lasting change if that client requires that clarification.

Suppose no clarification is necessary because they have a healthy amount of intent. After all, smokers do witness more negatives about smoking than positives. In that case, a rolled-up newspaper could easily do the trick if they so believe in the ultimate healing power of a swift but caring whack across the head with the local rag. A rapid change in habits is also scientifically observed with the placebo of sugar pills, no less.

The placebo effect is a well-established psychological phenomenon that creates rapid changes within the brain and body through thought alone. Joe Dispenza explains a double-blind experiment held by The UCLA Neuropsychiatric Institute to test a new antidepressant drug (Effexor). Of the fifty-one participants, roughly half were given a placebo.

All had an EEG (electroencephalograph) to measure brain wave activity during the experiment. After eight weeks, the study revealed thirty-eight percent of the placebo group reported feeling significantly better, including a full recovery from suicidal thoughts from one subject. Dispenza also explained that the EEG results after the trial showed an increase in the prefrontal cortex activity, which is responsible for cognition, that generally has low activity in patients who suffer from depression.

The results concluded how the placebo (sugar pills) not only changed the subject's ability to maintain a positive attitude and suppress suicidal thoughts, the placebo altered the brain's physical biology, and this was reported to continue several years later.

"The study results would soon show that thirty-eight percent of the placebo group felt better, compared to fifty-two percent of the group who received Effexor." - Dispenza

Dispenza discusses another placebo experiment by Dr Mosley, combining ten men who underwent knee surgery. Five men had the incisions made and were sown backup without the surgery to test the placebo effect after a physical surgery.

Two only had their knee joint cleaned, and the remaining had the complete surgery where the knee joint was scraped of cartilage.

The results reported back from the patients were the same; all ten men reported less pain and increased knee mobility. The pretend surgery yielded as much success as the actual surgery and continued to improve when reviewed six months later. In 2002 Dr Mosley performed the same experiment. This time with 180 volunteers producing the same results. Two years later, the volunteers were reviewed to observe the placebo group make a full recovery, having received a fake surgery.

"After the surgery, all ten of the patients in the study reported greater mobility and less pain." - Dispenza

The Power of the
Spoken Word

When engaging with clients, a healthy mindfulness of our vocabulary and its associations can drastically improve a client's desired outcome. For instance, I never miss the opportunity when a client arrives at my office. The chairs in my practice are equal in stature, and either one can belong to me and are positioned like that on purpose to make an impact. When I suggest my clients to sit in the chair that's going to help them make the most progress, on a few occasions, I have witnessed clients choose a chair, sit, ponder for a second, then ask to change chairs. I smile as I know this means they are deciding how successful they want to be, as the seat is now associated with that outcome.

When we are ill, instead of describing the illness when asked, which is continuing the behaviour of suffering from the illness, we can change that vocabulary, and instead, simply reply, 'I'm healing.'

When we write a word, it's called spelling because it is a spell we are creating. When you write a 'to-do list,' it's no secret how much more productive we are. Our internal dialogue is critical to a healthy and peaceful life, and negotiating with our thoughts is an essential skill to remain aware of. It's estimated we have between 50 and 60,000 thoughts per day. How many do you think are positive and inspiring from a place of love or fear? If we become the observer, we can monitor which side those thoughts land. Being aware is the first step in the process of change.

Intentions and meaning also play a significant role in how our body responds to an event. Research has concluded that the same experience repeated but with a different intention can change an individual's biological response, creating a different physical and mental outcome.

Dispenza describes this with research from Harvard by psychologist Alia Crum, Ph.D. A double-blind test with eighty-four maids examined the variation of how the maids perceived their daily working routine and if a change in their perception could influence their body chemistry to influence health benefits in line with regular exercise. Both groups were asked if they participated in regular exercise and sixty-seven replied not regularly, and thirty-seven percent did not exercise at all.

The control group was told their daily activities were in line with the surgeon general's recommended daily amount of exercise, which is thirty minutes - and by doing their job, they are positively influencing their health. The second group was monitored and not encouraged with relevant fitness facts correlating their daily activity to their health upkeep. Thirty days later, without any additional duties or exercise, the control group has lost an average of two pounds each, lowering their body fat and blood pressure.

"A placebo can come in many forms, a pill, suggestion, a test, procedure or a well-versed health care provider who understands the power of the spoken word." - Dispenza

Placebo and Authority Figures

Dr Kachmann describes how changing his vocabulary slightly before a minor surgical treatment influences a positive response and negates pain. Dr Kachmann explains how both nocebo and placebo effects are significantly increased in different situations, for instance, attending a doctor's appointment or having a conversation with a person of authority like a surgeon; because we trust to be guided by professionals to resolve critical situations.

The greater our perception of a situation, the more the hypothalamus pumps out hormones, which makes the body respond by receiving stimulating hormones such as adrenaline. Kachmann explains how a person of authority can create a placebo or nocebo by simply changing their vocabulary. Using a spinal tap as an example, spinal fluid is extracted from the spinal cord by inserting a long needle into the spine.

By carefully choosing the right words, Dr Kachmann could perform the procedure without pain and the need for anaesthetic by removing the word needle from the conversation. Dr Kachmann only suggested using anaesthetic by saying the sentence, "I'm going to numb you now," so the patient would have the idea of what to expect, trusting the doctor.

The relief came from the belief that signals the patient's subconscious mind to ensure a pain-free experience and the extraction finished without the patient realising. Dr Kachmann estimated they did over twenty thousand spinal taps this way by shifting the patients' perception.

"Placebos and nocebos are more effective in meaningful situations."
- Dr Kachmann

Reinventing Yourself

Imagine a child in their innocence for a few moments, unable to judge or comprehend their environment but open to all influence and education. They do not know how or why they should someday evaluate that information. They have zero ability to discern what information could later cause harm in their future. This child is a clean slate apart from any genetic abnormalities, of which the environment is now known to also influence.

Now, imagine how this child's local environment, school, and friends influence this child's character and personality, moulding their views and moral compass without their knowledge. The result, in many cases, is a life without purpose, knowing there is more to life but unsure what is required to fill that void to feel complete. Children are not taught how intuition works; therefore, their greatest skill is never fully nurtured or activated unless by chance. Not using our intuition is like having an invisible antenna connected to an abundance of wisdom, that's only turned on by mistake from time to time.

Albert Einstein once said, *"Insanity is doing the same thing over and over again and expecting different results."*

The dichotomy is this; A feeling to progress in life is prevented by not having any experience as to what direction to go in—no previous knowledge of how to progress, leaving the intellect confused about how to act. Intuition, unlike intellect, will offer a feeling of the future but no evidence of the destination and is considered abstract as opposed to a trusted previous experience.

The mistake is not knowing how to differentiate between the two, intuition and analytical thinking. The back and forth between the two states almost certainly results in feeling overwhelmed, not knowing which one to trust. Trusting intuition also takes a degree of belief, and if no previous attempts have been made to trust intuition, the trust in that feeling is minimal. Unless it is in your destiny, in that case, the feeling to act fills you with unparalleled determination.

Self-discovery is the single most liberating and creative exercise an individual can embark on. It also requires a large helping of forgiveness and compassion for who you used to be, as that was your conditioning, not your authentic self.

Writing this section reminds me of a book called *Jonathan Livingston Seagull*, by author Richard Bach. The book had a simple story with a profound message, we can all be so much more than we believe. A seagull called Jonathan is bored with mundane life. He finds a new passion for flight, and pushes himself to learn everything about flying. His increasing reluctance to conform results in his expulsion from the flock. This story is about finding passion and leading by example, it's a great story I won't tell you anymore.

The first step to reinvent yourself is being conscious of who you are.

The second step is acknowledging there is a missing part to your life. You may seem odd to those around you who are content in the same life whilst you feel unsettled. Finding the right person to discuss your thoughts may take a few false starts. Search for a person who has already reinvented themselves instead of those revolving in the same place in their life journey as you were. Modelling the success of others can speed up the process.

We will discuss the third step at the end of the book because a different type of knowledge is required. Understanding how to transition from instinct to intellect followed by intuition and why the last phase, intuition, is critical in optimum thinking and daily direction.

Dispenza discusses how our brain structure and neural network are formed throughout our lifetime from memories as we experience life — confirming one of the functions of our brain as the hard drive to our lives. This hard drive function makes our past a predominant part of our lives, leading to a large portion of society repeating the same trends and habits without being aware of an alternative. The continued use of the mind's hard drive (the subconscious) prohibits intuition because the analytical brain checks for a previous experience, projecting that into the future as a possible outcome.

This feedback loop can restrict new possibilities and increase fears if the previous experience was negative. Very much like dopamine and the H&N hormones, only one can function at a time, so it is true of intuition and the analytical mind. Both thinking analytically and intuitively are as natural as breathing air; however, due to a lack of knowledge of intuition, many get overwhelmed when going back and forth between the two functions. Separating intuition and the analytical mind is a skill that takes a dedicated time to master. The more you use your intuition and trust in the outcome, the greater it will become.

Dispenza explains this habitual action means our outer world controls our inner world, and the process is unconscious. We can be daydreaming through life, unaware of how we have allowed the environment to programme our minds. Each thought we have either reinforces neurotransmitters or creates new ones. There are only two options. However, from a thought, a chemical protein is made by the hypothalamus, called a neuropeptide. When in the bloodstream, it interacts with the body to create various actions depending on the thought that created the protein; this is how the body feels. Dispenza remarks how the brain is also aware of the body's feelings, meaning there is a loop from thought to sensations from the body to mind.

This loop can work against us when the mind creates thoughts to increase certain emotions the body is used to feeling. Dispenza refers to these neuropeptides as "molecules of emotion," each one is like a key floating in the bloodstream with its unique electromagnetic energy imprint.

When the key finds the right receptor site (lock), and when both are matching, the cells in the body now make the correct protein to create the correlating hormones to match the thought. *"Now you can understand that each time you've interacted with your external world, those events have shaped and moulded who you are today."*

Dispenza discusses how learning and being willing to change can lead to the death of your old personality. Which leads to psychological, biological, and neurological changes. He elaborates that when we decide to change, there is an initial discomfort as new choices, thoughts, and behaviours don't initially align with our body's chemistry and physical reactions.

Change is unchartered territory, making it easy to return to old habits because they are familiar. However, Dispenza highlights that growth doesn't happen in the comfort zone. Stepping back into the old is comfortable, making it easy to regress and receive the same old emotions and chemical reactions. Dispenza continues to say if we can persist outside our comfort zone and welcome the discomfort, we can deconstruct our old self on a cerebral level, and our bodies will change on a cellular level, too.

"The old self has to die for a new one to be reborn. Of course, that feels uncomfortable!" - Dispenza

Dispenza states it's our conscious choice to change our beliefs, thoughts, and behaviours and reinforce continuity and repetition that makes new chemicals feel normal. New experiences drive these new chemical reactions. He concludes that a new thought creates a new body as new genes make different proteins that change how the body reacts and interacts with life. *"As the new self is born, we must be biologically different, too."*

Dr Kachmann explains, what makes each person an individual is their unique response to events. As individuals interpret their reality, the autonomic nervous system responds, meaning it's a set response and activated by the subconscious mind, therefore not a conscious act.

If a person is pessimistic, without igniting a conscious thought, the subconscious mind will use each of the senses to interpret the external events depending on the history of similar events and make them part of our internal reality. Therefore, creating a bias towards events that are aligned with previous experiences. Previous habits will start a chain reaction from mind to body to exhibit a nocebo or placebo action. A nocebo or placebo response can be sparked in many situations, by a procedure, taking a pill, or as simple as constructing or deconstructing conversations with a practitioner or doctor, leading to healing or harm to the body. *"Your brain interprets the event, consciously or subconsciously, and the autonomic nervous system goes to work producing a stress or relaxation response."*

We are constantly at the mercy of old habits and reactions. Consciousness is the only action that can either prevent or adjust an old behaviour. How conscious are you of your habits, thoughts, and actions? And more importantly, which actions are you unaware of that no longer serve a useful purpose?

One afternoon after a session, I started a casual conversation with a client who worked as a waitress. When enquiring into her work routine, she commented that she never received tips from groups of ladies, only men. I suggested that was a self-fulfilling prophecy, and she could change that by changing what she expected.

I explained if she visualised each table with ladies giving her tips, that could be her new reality as that would change her physiology, facial expressions, body language, and the energy that she was projecting from a metaphysical perspective. The next time I saw her, she had a big smile and told me every table with ladies started tipping her and that she would carry on visualising her ideal outcome.

It's impressive; once we learn how the quantum field and the subconscious mind work, we can influence our lives exponentially. Prosperity is there for the taking if you believe and trust, leaving hope to be obsolete.

Free Will Explained

Michael Gazzaniga offers his insights into free will and its functions. Gazzaniga makes solid points from a philosophical standpoint and highlights how free will is, in fact, a choice that is created from one's conscious mind and not governed by any outside forces or supernatural entities.

Gazzaniga explains that other powerful feelings or compulsions that materialise from lack of control are within our ability to change. He mentions the famous conundrum presented when many people see a doughnut. This first reaction is always instinctual, that will taste good, as it's a desire that is programmed into the mind from the repetition of countless times enjoying different types of doughnuts or exchangeable for one's preferred treat. The choice comes from the reasoning, our responsibility for our health and wellbeing.

Free will is the variance between having a choice or following the programme and executing the habitual task.

"In traditional philosophy, free will is the belief that human behaviour is an expression of personal choice that is not determined by physical forces, fate, or God." - Gazzaniga

Gazzaniga discusses determinism and its limitations. It tries to predetermine events and actions by using variables to calculate an outcome, suggesting life is predictable.

Determinism is a philosophy. When referencing the past you can predict a present state using causal laws. Determinism is concluded from left-brained intellectual interpretations. Left without a counter argument would suggest humanity is not required to take responsibility for its actions, suggesting free will is an illusion.

"Determinism is the philosophical belief that all current and future events, actions, including cognition, decisions, and behaviour, are causally necessitated by preceding events combined with the laws of nature." - Gazzaniga

Gazzaniga explains free will with an experiment conducted by Kathleen Vohs and Jonathan Schooler, a psychology professor at the University of California. To test the hypothesis that if a person's sense of responsibility is changed, it contributes to their behaviour and view of their free will. Two batches of students were asked to take a test on a computer, and both sets of students were warned that the computer had a fault and automatically gave the correct answers, and to prevent this, they could press a certain key. The only difference between the two groups was the reading material before the test was taken. Group A read a passage from a book by Francis Crick, *The Astonishing Hypothesis* with a deterministic bias.

Group B read another book with a ‹positive outlook on life.’ The results were conclusive. Group A, influenced by the deterministic bias, cheated on the test, and Group B didn't. Gazzaniga summarised that the uncertainty of free will permitted cheating because it was pointless to resist or exercise any effort to apply their virtues.

"A psychology professor at the University of California has shown in a clever experiment that people act better when they believe they have free will." - Gazzaniga

Gazzaniga goes deeper into the subject of free will by using conclusions by The

University of Florida State and the department of social psychologists by Roy Baumeister, E. J. Masicampo, and C. Nathan DeWall. They concluded that individuals who read insignia into deterministic philosophers were prone to aggression and unwilling to assist when others needed help. They also observed that individuals who exhibit a selfish tendency need significant self-awareness to overcome selfishness or aggressive behaviour. The belief in free will is the vital ingredient to override what would be unconscious actions.

"People prefer not to bother because bothering, in the form of self-control, requires exertion and depletes energy." - *Gazzaniga*

Why Beliefs are Only Safe
if Left Unchallenged

Jillian was one of my one-time clients with a phobia of counting. Phobias are irrational beliefs not founded on logical knowledge but hold a great deal of dominance over individuals in different ways, depending on how the subconscious mind constructs the phobia or limiting belief.

Jillian was on holiday at a resort I was contracted to in Thailand; one afternoon, Jillian appeared and inquired if I could help her and continued to explain how counting and using numbers was a daunting experience for her. She explained that even counting her exchanged funds at a bank could bring on an anxious feeling and make her nervous. Without realising I was using my sensory acuity, I could see, hear, feel as she talked. I was watching for any signs of micro expressions that express guilt or fear. I work from a place of minimal triggers, the path of least resistance.

I was getting enough eye contact, and her posture was open to suggest there was no trauma associated with the event that caused this phobia. I always ask when clients think their limitations start, and her reply was, "Some time when she was young." As she replied, her voice was steady and at a regular pitch that satisfied my inquiry. She asked if I could help, straight away, I knew a regression coupled with some inner child work would be a suitable technique to explore this challenge.

During the session when Jillian was in her altered state of awareness, we progressed to the event, where she struggled during a math exam. Jillian expressed how hopeless she felt and knew she would fail. She saw herself putting her arms on the desk and dropping her head, giving up and wanting to sleep. This was the conclusion her younger self arrived at when Jillian was just ten years old. Jillian was now forty-three.

For thirty-three years, Jillian had the same conclusion, and it was a disability she carried with her influencing and restricting her skill to engage with mathematics. When we started the inner child work, Jillian's younger version was in a place of anxiety, trapped in a cycle of beginning a test and never feeling whole enough to complete it. I encouraged Jillian to reframe that event with her younger version, empowering her and asking if that state served a useful purpose.

Towards the end of the session, still supporting Jillian, holding that space, viewing what she tells me so I, too, can be part of that process from a quantum field perspective, there was a long silence. These moments are unique because it's in the silence where all the changes take place. I knew the deep work had now begun, the subconscious computing of her quantum world that no science had been able to comprehend.

After a few more minutes, I saw a single tear roll down Jillian's face, and a smile suddenly appeared. I knew the work was complete. I asked Jillian, "And as you see your younger self, what difference can you see?" She replied that she was happy now, smiling and acting like a little girl.

The question was open-ended. It could have gone either way, meaning the work might not be finished. All sessions are a three-way process between me as the facilitator, my client's consciousness, and their subconscious mind.

As a 'belt and braces job,' I asked Jillian to ask her younger self, "Before we go, can she use the same power but this time to help you?" And I waited in silence. Jillian smiled and said, "She replied, yes." The third person reply also indicates genuine inner child work.

The session ended organically when Jillian and her subconscious mind were both ready. I bought her back to full waking consciousness and gave Jillian a glass of water so the residue of that altered state would dispense faster as her mind and body reconnected.

Jillian came back to Thailand the year after and searched me out. I remember this like yesterday because she had the biggest smile on her face like she was bursting to tell me something. She was a tall mixed heritage lady whose aura and personality were larger than life, so I recognised her immediately when I felt that energy in my vicinity.

Her opening line was, "Do you remember me?" Which always makes me smile because I have an excellent long-term memory. She explained how much the session changed her thinking and said, "Guess what?" - I played along, and she said, "I bought a restaurant and guess what my favourite part of the business is?"

It was one of those rhetorical moments, so I just smiled, and she replied, "Standing on the till and cashing out the customers." We both laughed. It's those moments that are like being paid again but with energy the second time.

Toch explains how core beliefs are learned from those in our environment when we are young. As a child, we don't question how we are conditioned, however in later years, those same beliefs may be examined when new experiences bring questions about one's reality.

Toch describes how inconsistencies in our lives become visible when our beliefs don't correlate with our reality, using the most prominent belief as an example, wealth and status. We all need money to live in this 3rd dimension; however, few call it the route to all evil. If such a belief is endorsed as a child, both beliefs may confront each other in adulthood as one requires money to live, but a parallel belief can give the feeling it's also going to cause a disadvantage.

Toch continues to clarify how such beliefs can restrict adults from changing if they have been constantly conditioned, and those beliefs are close to a reality they may experience, and the holes of truth are not so far apart. It's highly predictable for an adult to defend beliefs and ignore any new evidence they might find. Toch concludes that beliefs can be left unchecked or not evaluated if the outer world does not conflict with those beliefs. However, because reality rarely is consistent with other people's views of the world, what one experiences isn't absolute, making said beliefs questionable in their inconsistency. *"The beliefs a person has acquired are safe as long as they are not put to the test."*

Imagine a young boy. We can call him Matt. Often Matt is sat at the table with his father as he reads a newspaper. The father talks out loud with what he thinks is a throwaway comment about how much footballers earn; "Look at that son, one million pounds a week, it's disgusting, isn't it?

Who needs that amount of money, ay son? Money is the root of all evil anyway."

The father is set in his ways with no ambition to earn more than he requires. The father repeats the same verses he heard from a poor working-class family as a child, so the 'poor mindset' continues.

Matt grows into a man and works hard at the same company embracing the same strong work ethic his father conditioned into him. One year, Matt is called into the manager's office and offered a promotion with double the responsibility and a significant salary increase.

Matt is delighted as consciously he knows how that extra income will benefit him, but he has an internal conflict he cannot put his finger on. Over the next few weeks, his admired work ethic starts to lag, and he sabotages the opportunity. He is confused about why he is acting out. Matt doesn't remember the conditioning by his father, but his subconscious mind and its programmes are aligning Matt's reality on his behalf. This story highlights the same functions of the mind as the other client testimonials.

If we go back and add some internal conscious thought to Matt's mind while he is at the table, listening to his father;

For example:

"I'm going to be wealthy, dad; I'll show you. I'm not living poor anymore."

Or

"I love you, dad; I'm going to be rich and look after you, I promise".

With these empowering thoughts, what type of programmes do you think his subconscious mind would create?

The only difference is how conscious Matt is of his environment and his internal representation of his world. Matt conditioned his mind; he was the master of his Universe.

What kind of conditioning did you receive as a child regarding money? Worth a thought or two?

Psychosomatic Effects and Secondary Gain

The subconscious mind is the powerhouse of our reality, and pain can be psychosomatic, meaning created in the mind and transferred to the body. Pain has one function: telling the mind there is a fault in the body and restricting movement, depending on how severe the damage. However, there is primary pain and secondary pain. Primary pain is from the autonomic nervous system, a feedback loop that informs the mind from the body. Secondary pain is the conscious mind's interpretation of events, assuming levels of pain and severity.

Taking this model further, the secondary gain is manufacturing pain or disability to receive emotional compensation.

One afternoon, at the printers, speaking with the owner, she informed me of a friend from Israel with arthritis in his knees. I enquired further, and his story started with him suffering from arthritis in the UK, and he had moved to warmer climates to alleviate that pain, which worked initially.

It transpired that Simon was now in the UK because a doctor had suggested so many different medicines attempting to fix the problem that he ended up in hospital with internal bleeding. Subsequently, he came back to the UK to get further treatment. How Simon's arthritis reappeared gave the clue it was secondary gain.

When Simon went to Israel many years ago, his pain miraculously disappeared, and he lived a healthy life. As a

British citizen, his Hebrew skills were verbally developing, but his written skills were lagging, which meant his ability to attain work was restricted to manual labour.

After living in Israel for many years, he settled down and started a family; this naturally incurs extra costs and highlighted his limited income causing financial problems causing difficulties in his relationship. On a conscious level, he knew his work options were limited, and I can only presume the cycle of needing more income, not solving that problem, led to the subconscious mind stepping in to relieve the anguish. When I heard the story, I concluded secondary gain and offered to help.

After the first consultation, we immediately started a subconscious realignment session; however, it was early on in my career, and I made a mistake and didn't check if he completed the metaphor.

A few days later it dawned on me, as I was walking through a shopping centre in Manchester, and my curiosity got the better of me, so I called Simon and asked how he completed the metaphor; he replied, "I didn't."

I was astounded at his reply and asked if he had noted any change in his arthritis, and he replied, "Not much." He inquired if that was important, and I told him, "It was the most important part of the session, and you didn't take the opportunity to make progress."

I didn't charge for the session, so in my mind, there was no value in my service. I told him, "That was a shame," we ended the call. I was marginally frustrated at the time.

A few minutes later, Simon called again and asked, "Can I have another session." I thought about the previous session and why it wasn't successful and replied, "I don't think it will work." He was shocked and asked why. I replied, "Because you had the opportunity to let go and didn't take it."

I only have one tool, and that's my voice and direction. If he didn't want to follow my direction, there isn't much more I can do to help; it's that simple. We ended the call. Simon swiftly called me back and said he was sorry and pleaded for another session, I could hear the sincerity in his voice and knew the level of intent was now high enough, so I agreed.

The day of the session, I remember watching him hobble up the stairs to my third-floor apartment; he was taking his time, cautious with every step. I could see he was in pain. This time the session was different, he didn't hold back, and he completed the metaphor. It was a long process of which I had all the patience in the world because it takes as long as it takes.

I knew this time Simon was committed; I could feel it; at the time, I couldn't describe what I felt. I just knew. It was early in my career, in 2006. I didn't know the full extent of the Oneness or how to describe it or its functions, but I had an instinct to utilise it, and my understanding grew from there.

In the session, I was with Simon every step of the way, matching his newfound enthusiasm to heal with my ability to be the observer of his transformation. When he returned to full waking consciousness, he struggled to open his eyes, not because I gave him a double bind as I did with the man in the airport. My technique wasn't as polished back then as it is now. But because he has been in a super-deep state of internal processing.

He knew he had connected to a deeper part of himself, and I was there to witness that connection. We were both pleased.

In hindsight, my lack of experience was also a factor in his first session. If I had the experience, I should have checked, but it led him to come back with a new level of intent. That situation was meant to be.

We arranged another visit in a week, and he left. A week later, once again after he buzzed my intercom, I left my apartment and waited at the landing but this time to see him spring up the stairs like a man in his twenties. I was amazed, and he had the biggest smile on his face. I said, "Feeling better then?". He was also surprised at his progress in such a short span of time.

This session inspired me to push the boundaries in my work and was just another reason to trust in the immense power of the mind and know if we believe we can achieve, we can.

Aitchison clarifies how disempowering beliefs (AKA limiting beliefs) can cause physical and mental distress with variations in severity. Aitchison alludes to how limiting beliefs control our reality and restrains individuals from their achievements.

Aitchison also explains how beliefs are either empowering or disempowering, and how awareness provides us with a choice. The choice to cultivate more empowering beliefs that serve and encourage us to live a balanced life. Aitchison notes how disempowering beliefs can cause illness or disease within the body as our thoughts are psychosomatic. He explains the extreme ramifications of holding negative beliefs and how they are not mutually exclusive to damaging the body or the mind. *"Disempowering beliefs hold us back from truly living a life of fullness and wellness and can even cause us physical and mental harm if we don't recognise them and acknowledge them."*

Beliefs Restrict Communication

We have all done things we are not proud of; that's part of growing and evolving. Our conditioned beliefs can be overwhelmingly impulsive, especially regarding religion or what we believe in strongly.

As a professional facilitator, I've found a way to accept all religious beliefs of others, so they work to complement a session instead of being a point of contention. Putting a client first and being in a state of acceptance is essential; it doesn't matter if an individual wears a Star of David or a Crucifix. If we work from the view that all religions have something good to offer, we can overcome such bigoted ways.

The media did a fantastic job at turning nations against one religion, the Muslim faith. There are extremists in every faith, and this one instance stopped me in my tracks. I was crossing the border from Thailand to Myanmar by a river in a long tail boat. There was an American chap sat across from me as we chugged down the river, and we started chatting about local affairs.

This gentleman pointed up into the hills and asked if I knew of the Buddhist monks killing in the name of Buddha. I nearly fell off the side of the boat in shock as I had no evidence of such extremism in the Buddhist religion because I had only been conditioned that some Muslims were extreme. However, just a minute fraction of the Muslim faith chooses to misinterpret scriptures to suit their own beliefs.

In that conversation, many contradictory ideas of human rights and peaceful religions were being deconstructed in my mind; I almost didn't want to believe what I was hearing. I later researched the facts to confirm what I was told.

If the mainstream media chose to highlight these few monks and repeatedly conditioned society with the monks' actions, would society then develop an aversion to that culture? Most generalisations and assumptions are dangerous because they are based on small amounts of information or instances and are considered accurate.

Working in Asia has enabled me to travel extensively to China, Singapore, Malaysia, Burma, Vietnam, and Indonesia. I've also visited many predominantly Muslim countries and found some of the most honest and gentle human beings in proportion to any western country. After having those new experiences, my perception of others and their beliefs opened. I have reasoned with any extremist factions that have been at the forefront of my mind because of the media, as everyone deserves the chance to prove themselves as an individual. Guess what. I've not regretted that yet.

In 2009, I enrolled in a course to study as a naturopath; my attempt to pass the first year of biology and medicine was futile; the material was a little too cerebral for my brain. However, I did form a lasting relationship with the most unusual person. Abdul is a traditional Muslim who rolls up his trousers above his ankles, has a long beard, follows his devout religious beliefs, and prays five times a day.

If you saw Abdul and I together and tried to comprehend our friendship, your mind would probably prolapse out of your ear from attempting to consider what we have in common as friends. Nevertheless, Abdul is one of my favourite people, and I have had many open, honest conversations enriching both of our lives. When I travel back to the UK, he is always on the top of my list of people to meet and catch up with, and I enjoy listening to his wisdom.

Our initial shared interest was in nutrition as we were both studying naturopathic medicine, and later, we discovered we have many other similar views and ideas, which strengthened our relationship. Many years into our friendship, we were at a coffee shop, and he started a statement with, "In my religion..." And in my ignorance, I stopped him and said, "Abdul, I'm not interested in discussing the Muslim faith, but I respect your views." That did not faze him, and our conversation continued.

On reflection, was I so unsure in my faith that my deep respect for Abdul may leave me open to his conditioning, or was I already conditioned by society about the Muslim faith and didn't want to hear any other information because I would have to re-evaluate my conditioning? It was probably the latter, or maybe I didn't want any religion getting into the way of our friendship as it is a contentious subject. Reviewing other previous friendships, I've had good friendships with others that had held faith in high regard and always felt curious about their views, from Judaism, Hinduism to the Sikh religion.

It wasn't until four or five years later, having lived abroad longer and better travelled, that I inadvertently revised my beliefs, which rightfully required adjustments. Then I was able to shed my conditioning and grow from that limited place. Looking back, I understand how my attitude was closed, and since then, Abdul has shared insights into his faith, and I have listened to what resonated with me. I am now wise enough to understand that accepting other religions doesn't mean you are not loyal to your ideas. Our friendship has grown, and we remain good friends. Consequently, what that experience taught me was how powerful the "I am" statement can be.

What Osho elegantly explains about beliefs is how restrictive many are and how conditioning by our environment, friends, family, the media, etc., is mainly responsible for our beliefs. Osho highlights how beliefs can break down communications between individuals who are not conditioned by the same environment and uses religion as a case in point. Osho adds that beliefs can be a burden making us biased and unable to take in new or alternative facts because holding two opposing beliefs simultaneously is a challenge. By making beliefs so rigid or a hard crust as Osho would describe, such beliefs are difficult to change, and adapting to new circumstances or different views can be limiting, making communication a burden.

Osho mentions strong beliefs are like "living in prison." Ironically, we have the key but unaware, especially when others surround us in a similar prison, so the beliefs seem to be routine and unchallenged. Osho adds that such beliefs can create fear and negative emotions that damage the body and mind, hindering personal evolution. Osho continues that any sentence beginning with "I am" is from a belief and restricts our development from expanding into more. He alludes to the fact that the "I am" statements confirm our identity.

This is a dangerous position because any connection to that identity that is threatened subjectively, objectively, or indirectly to your independent being can also be perceived as an attack—leaving any groups, religions, or social systems open to affecting your wellbeing and general health. Osho concludes that not knowing is the opposite of beliefs. Being in that space of not knowing means we are essentially open to all dialogue with others and, therefore, for new experiences.

Osho has committed to the stance that beliefs are the downfall of humanity and essentially destroy the Oneness, the communion of humanity. Osho describes how letting go of the belief systems creates more space to explore life not bound but free from expectations or presumptions with a reverted sense of innocence and mystery of the world. Instead of arrogance towards new experiences. This, in turn, increases the sense of mystery in life, not knowing what to expect and being open to explore and experience new adventures.

Osho comments on other philosophies, such as Sufis and Zen masters who also explore and enjoy the unknown feeling of being free from the burden of beliefs.

"Dialogue disappears when you are burdened with belief systems." - Osho

The Nicotine Myth
Founded on False Beliefs

Psychotherapist Chris Holmes explains how beliefs prohibit an individual's ability to change habits and how complex compulsive habits retain beliefs that support actions; as opposed to simple habits with no beliefs attached.

For instance, smokers believe smoking will calm them down, however, Holmes clarifies the British Medical Dictionary's explanation of nicotine's physical effects and how it increases a smoker's heart rate, which is the opposite of calming. Holmes also comments how the British Medical Dictionary states how nicotine restricts the arteries, increasing blood pressure. Combining both high blood pressure and increased heart rate merged with stress is known to promote heart attacks and strokes.

Heart failure certainly doesn't sound very relaxing. Reverting the belief that nicotine is relaxing is pure unadulterated propaganda promoted by advertising companies. Who, incidentally, were paid to market cigarettes to the public—leaving smokers with a complex compulsive habit because those beliefs require deconstructing before a smoker's so called "addiction" can be resolved.

Holmes continues that the core belief connected to smoking is the fantasy of pleasure, and it's that smoking is enjoyable. You may be reading that statement with an internal running commentary of disbelief; hold your horses before you gallop to a common conclusion. Later I'll give you an exercise you can use with a smoker that proves his point. The unsuspecting smoker won't be pleased with your insights, but it might be entertaining for you if you are partial to some humour.

Holmes highlights that this one belief of pleasure overrides a smoker's consciousness as their awareness is focused on other matters, so the horrific effects of smoking are hidden in the present as smokers project their mind into the future or back into the past. While a simple habit such as nail-biting is a stress response, there is no pleasure attached or reward or beliefs supporting the behaviour; it's an anxiety reaction.

Holmes comments that smokers may also crave a cigarette as a programmed knee-jerk reaction to anxiety or stress; however, the smoker is under the impression that nicotine provides some relief when in fact, nicotine compounds stress. One of the conditioned beliefs developed by advertising companies and passed down through the generations is, 'I'm stressed, I'm going for a smoke,' the popular saying that's compounded society's belief systems to override the terrible effects of nicotine.

"Nail biting is another simple compulsive habit, with no beliefs supporting the behaviour." - Holmes

The reasons young adults start smoking have nothing to do with nicotine but other psychological benefits. The five main reasons are:

1. To be accepted by a group, build rapport
2. To look cool
3. To look older
4. To be rebellious
5. To try something new

The repetition and consistency combined with the indoctrination about nicotine creates a complex compulsive habit, also incorrectly known as the ‹smoking addiction›. Nicotine is a poison and under 60mg can kill a man and has no other medical applications, categorically, zero. Off the top of my head, I can think of two successful drug trials to treat cancer and candida that started off treating animals for parasite infestations, no less.

Splenda or Sucralose was initially developed as an insecticide by two British scientists, but still, no other nicotine applications.

Dr Edward Shepherd explains how one in eight babies are born prematurely in the United States and how Viagra stimulates premature babies' hearts:

"Another adult drug we use to help premature babies that is surprising to most people is called sildenafil, which is more commonly known as Viagra."

If nicotine was a drug, why do smokers take off nicotine patches to smoke? If you are not laughing at that statement, you can check with a smoker who probably for a short time tried patches and can collaborate that fact. The delivery system doesn't matter for any other drug; a heroin addict will smoke, inject, even chew heroin. However, nicotine only works when smoked.

If nicotine was as addictive as people say, why aren't students addicted to nicotine patches before exams? They are smart enough to acquire other children's Ritalin but haven't worked out the calming effects from nicotine patches. Or is that the next new trend? I doubt it because the patches make you feel ill; that's my personal experience and evidence from fellow ex-smokers.

Imagine for a moment you are at a party. It's your turn to do the alcohol run, there are two smokers in the group, and you ask for their preferred brands, however at the store, you see nicotine patches, how do you think they will respond when you get back to the party and offer them the alternative delivery system for nicotine. You know the answer, and it's connected to the five reasons they started smoking in the first place, no one looks cool and acts rebellious with a patch on their arm.

Drug addicts are known to break into veterinarian facilities to steal drugs that mimic heroin; why don't druggies steal nicotine patches if they are an effective delivery system.

Have you stood outside a 7-Eleven and had a teenager ask you for some cigarettes? And after you said 'no,' they replied, "Oh, a box of nicotine patches will be fine, too!" Never have those words been uttered by a fifteen-year-old who stood outside a 7-Eleven harassing its patrons.

My final question is this. If nicotine is the drug we are meant to believe it is, why isn't there a black market for nicotine patches or gum, and why don't people get addicted? Because nicotine isn't a drug, and it's not addictive. What we believe about nicotine requires updating, especially if an individual wants to stop smoking because the current beliefs are trapping smokers in the repetitive cycle of attempting to give up.

If you have a smoker friend and you want to help them, here is a simple question that's designed to bring original conscious thought to their habit.

It's advisable to ask this question with an extremely pleasant pre-frame accompanied by a soft and enquiring voice (I'm smiling as I write this because I've done the opposite, and sensitive smokers under their spell won't be amused at all.)

I'm curious as I watch you smoke that cigarette; I trust I'm not disturbing you?

May I ask you a question?

The general reply is yes, mainly because they have no idea what is coming next, and I can guarantee, by the time they comprehend your question, they are going to wish you hadn't asked it!

What is the enjoyment in smoking that cigarette?

If they reply with what they are also doing, like it's nice with a coffee or helps them think, that's the conditioning and not true. Carbon monoxide reduces oxygen to the brain, restricting cognitive function, certainly not increasing it!

Carefully bring them back to the cigarette and say:

That's what you are doing while smoking. I mean, precisely what are you enjoying about smoking that cigarette?

This is the dangerous part. If they are conscious enough, they will notice it's disgusting and put it out. Or they feel so silly they will defend the action.

You can press further if you dare and say, is it the smell that stays with you for hours on end or the tightening of your chest, the tastes it leaves in your mouth?

At that point, you have broken a spell that's been with them from their early days of smoking and attached to the five reasons they started in the first place. They cannot un-ring that bell. When I teach my students how to help their clients stop smoking, the first half of the session is focused on conscious awareness of the smoker's actions; I'm also amused to watch how many of the students who smoke wrestle with these indisputable facts, as I did when I became conscious of the spell I was also under when I was a smoker.

If you are a smoker and wish to give up, although we have covered a few of the myths here, many more require deconstructing before you can shut down the cravings once and for all.

Once you know how and why you started smoking on a conscious level, it's possible to communicate that to the subconscious mind for realignment. It's impossible to quit without the subconscious mind being informed, and the consequences are probably familiar.

A repetition of stopping and starting;

- Replacing smoking with another habit, leaving the smoking cravings active
- Finding it hard to resist smoking when drinking coffee or alcohol
- Feeling overwhelmed when stressed because you are restrained from smoking
- Struggling to be around smokers months or years after you have quit
- Putting on excess weight because the smoking craving is being confused with a craving for food
- A generally feeling of irritability

The good news is, once your subconscious and conscious mind are on the same page, all the above issues go away. That was my experience and that of many hundreds of clients I assisted in shutting down their cravings.

If you stopped smoking months or years ago with free will, I'm afraid the subconscious mind that holds your smoking program still thinks you are a smoker.

If you have started questioning the smoking habit and attempted to quit, you are in an excellent place to make rapid progress.

Follow the link below to enrol in our free quit smoking program.

www.anthonyaugustine.co.uk/quit

Dopamine, the Molecule of More

While our beliefs are undoubtedly conditioned and installed by the environment, there is a subtle internal process that guides and coerces our thoughts, ensuring our survival through procreation by influencing desires.

Lieberman explains how the mesolimbic pathway (AKA the dopamine desire circuit) controls the body's dopamine and its effects. Dopamine is nature's helping hand to ensure humanity moves forward; however, it is a double-edged sword when feeling compelled to react to specific environmental triggers. Or constantly evaluating what resources may be required to survive or procreate, which could be a mistake to unconsciously act on.

While food is just an option to consider, the dopamine hit from high sugar and fat foods may not feel like an option but a necessary action. The same is true for an individual's sexual attraction to another. *"The sensation of wanting is not a choice you make. It is a reaction to the things you encounter."*

The greatest challenge for humans is being present in the moment; this is remarkably more difficult with the enchantment of technology. A mobile phone having hundreds of applications can draw our attention for many hours a day, flicking between emails, Facebook, Twitter, and so on.

The 'present' is called such because it's a gift. We strive for more so we can enjoy the fruits of our labour. However, due to the functions of habits and the powerful dopamine hormone, wanting can become habitual. The fruits we strive for are not eaten when they arrive but often passed by for the next, even greater flavours promised by the future.

Hence the term, the grass is always greener on the other side. The proverbial fence is a sign of wanting now what others have worked hard for, a result of not fully comprehending how gratitude works. Gratitude is a word like no other in the dictionary. Unlike other words, the consequences of a lack of gratitude are metaphysically unparalleled.

Gratitude is one of the golden keys to numerous doors to the Quantum realm. The key to gratitude is found in the present moment, mysteriously hidden from the past or future. The key is a gift from the present as a present, but receiving the key doesn't mean you know where the lock is found. Finding the lock is a skill. We see the door by closing our physical eyes and opening the intuitive eye to all inner realms of higher awareness.

When we use the key of gratitude, we can step out of our tiny construct to discover the endless ocean of high vibrating consciousness, the frequency of the unknowable, to bring a little of that back. Gracefully reminding us we are but a flash of life in an eternal cycle of energy beyond time and space that we don't have the mental capacity to comprehend, living with amnesia of our true potential. Receiving the key is your God-given right. Learning to use the key is a choice! How many of those moments per day do you deserve? All it takes is a moment of your precious time.

Often, individuals with a steady work ethic reach their desired level of success but can feel something is missing from their life. This void is due mainly to a lack of gratitude in the fullest expression of the word. Intellectual appreciation doesn't begin to scratch the surface of what is required to reprogramme the mind with gratitude. Metaphysical gratitude transforms the mind into an unparalleled quantum state necessary to translate the concept into a powerful feeling of being; that creates profoundly inspired actions.

One afternoon I was coaching a Hollywood movie producer whose films were graced with an actress such as Angelina Jolie. For privacy purposes, we will use the name Thomas. He described how he never had any excitement when celebrating the wrap-up of a movie. Thomas's mind is one of perfection. He mentioned how he drove his crew to the edge on many occasions because he adjusted sets so often, being a perfectionist. He was successful; however, his mind was fuelled with dopamine, the excitement of the next challenge, the creative process, which is future paced not in the present moment. Meaning the completion of a film never met his expectations because the H&N hormones were not the same as the powerful dopamine fix, he unconsciously searched for.

One evening we were having dinner, chatting about the film industry, and he shared an even deeper level of perfection. Thomas described film sets and how some actors would need to read some lines they couldn't remember from boards discreetly placed around them as they were acting. Thomas described how frustrated he would get if actors blinked when a sentence comes to a comma.

I never noticed that before when watching movies. It's one of those instances that we miss because you didn't know they were there, but you see it all the time once you know. Now when watching a movie, I cannot help but observe if actors are reading from boards and if they blink when finishing a sentence with a comma.

To conclude, when we correlated Thomas's empty feeling to gratitude, Thomas was amazed at how he missed that subtle stage in completing a task and now understood why he struggled to celebrate at wrap up parties with his staff after completing a movie.

Mindfulness is centred around being present with ourselves and becoming aware. To stop and observe how our nature has evolved or devolved and make the adjustments accordingly. We can only do one at a time; it's impossible to be present and think about the future or reflect and reminisce in the past.

Only one state of being is achievable at once, as our consciousness has restricted functions. Being present brings meaning to life and our achievements. It's such a simple formula and mostly overlooked as a complicated task.

The nemesis of the present moment can be dopamine; as Lieberman postulates, this fascinating endocrine hormone ignites a sensation of excitement and plunges our thoughts into the future as it's our future imagination that boosts dopamine. Other future feelings like hope, anticipation and enthusiasm for the unexpected all fall into the category of future, imaginary possibilities.

Lieberman continues to explain the attachment the dopamine sensation can encourage in individuals to spend more time in the future, only thinking of the best outcome because dopamine is a feel-good hormone, as Thomas described. However, it's only a figment of the imagination; dopamine isn't interested in having things, that's irrelevant, only wanting things; making dopamine an aggressive anticipation molecule rather than a pleasure molecule, the desire circuit is powered by dopamine.

"Dopamine circuits don't process experience in the real world, only imaginary future possibilities." - Lieberman

Lieberman follows up by noting the opposite to dopamine is the H&N (Here and Now hormones) neurotransmitters that offer a present moment of pleasure and sensation as opposed to the excitement and anticipation sensation from dopamine which is future paced.

Lieberman adds that the collection of H&N hormones transition from dopamine to a steady, relaxing, and sustainable flow of serotonin, oxytocin, and endorphins hormones, also known as endocannabinoids; one is named after the Sanskrit word anandamide, translated to delight, joy, and bliss.

"Our brains must transition from future-oriented dopamine to present-oriented chemicals, a collection of neurotransmitters we call the Here and Now molecules, or the H&N's." - Lieberman

What an individual creates in their mind is an illusion; Lieberman explains wanting as a dopamine fuelled desire which is in the future from imagination. Once that becomes our reality, the perfect desire is often full of holes and doesn't match the construct formed in the imagination. Once the dopamine-driven thought becomes a reality, a separate set of hormones takes over to drive the experience, H&N hormones. H&N hormones are the opposite of dopamine that's constructed by the wanting phase, leaving reality to feel different than anticipated.

"Wanting and liking are produced by two different systems in the brain, so we often don't like the things we want." - Lieberman

Furthermore, Lieberman adds how the 'reward prediction error' works, the environment stimulates dopamine when unexpected events transpire. This also happens when something better than expected happens. When an individual's prediction is wrong, an unexpected burst of dopamine is excreted due to something new, exciting, and unexpected.

"When things become part of the daily routine, there is no more reward prediction error, and dopamine is no longer triggered to give you those feelings of excitement." - Lieberman

Lieberman explains an experiment with a rat highlighting how dopamine is influenced by anticipation and surprise. When food is randomly dropped into the cage, the animal has a dopamine surge; however, the dopamine stops if the rat is expecting food because the timing is consistent.

"If you drop a pellet of food into a rat's cage, the animal will experience a dopamine surge." - Lieberman

The balance in life comes from a balance of brain chemistry as Lieberman expands on how both dopamine and H&N neurotransmitters are designed to complement each other when used for their strengths. H&N neurotransmitters encourage feeling in the present moment and connecting to those around us with compassion and acceptance. The dark side of too much H&N is present moment indolence, irresponsible living a carefree lifestyle.

The dark side to a life driven by future possibilities is excessive dopamine. Still, too much is endless, always needing to achieve without satisfaction in the present and not enjoying the fruits of one's labour. The balance is to use dopamine to achieve and search for the mysteries of life, followed by the present moments of H&N continuing with the happiness circuit and being content.

"Dopamine and the H&N evolved to work together. They often act in opposition to one another, which helps maintain stability among constantly firing brain cells. In many instances, dopamine and H&N get thrown out of balance, especially on the dopaminergic side." - Lieberman

Lieberman explains that dopamine and the H&N hormones are designed to work together; however, individuals with dopamine production firing at a greater level, leads to unhappy achievers. Either hormone alone creates an unhealthy imbalance, and conscious awareness is required. When an individual loses sight of their internal balance, they are subject to influence from the outer world. Being lazy or an overachiever has consequences; an individual's actions or lack of them are signs of following too far on either side of the balance. The symptoms of such will be evident in an individual's character and personality.

"The modern world drives us to be all dopamine. Too much dopamine can lead to productive misery, while too much H&N can lead to happy indolence." - Lieberman

Lieberman uses mastery to bring his point home; dopamine is the driving force to achieve, each day we focus on what we want to achieve, see it in our mind's eye and feel what it will be like to be there, touch, smell and sense what we are working towards.

Dopamine fuels the journey and keeps an individual on track, pushing through challenging times with a taste of the future each time individuals project their image of themselves to the finish line. At that point, Lieberman explains how dopamine hands over the baton of the race to the H&N hormones to enrich the present experience to be masters of our reality.

For those individuals searching for greater contentment, Lieberman suggests a conscious awareness of their desires. To manage a balance between what they achieve, time spent in the future, the endless thirst for more, and move from dopamine to the 'Here & Now hormones' that enrich the present moment. He continues to elaborate that a complete performance of the mind and brain is the combination of both moving from creation to meaning, achieving and having the ability to enjoy, basking in the happiness that desires and aspirations lead towards.

"It takes both dopamine and H&N to attain happiness, the state of being that the philosopher Aristotle considered to be the goal of all other goals."
- Lieberman

The definition of free will has been a hot topic discussed by many philosophers, St. Augustine, Plato, Aristotle, and more. In the twentieth century, science is used to find a conclusion, fighting for both sides of the coin, a deterministic reality and one of free will. O'Connor explains how Plato's version of free will was to overcome the internal conflict and apply reason over desire. From what O'Connor describes of Plato's views, it seems Plato described a conscious observation of one's desires moving towards a place of personal development, using virtues that protect oneself from humanity's most raw basic instincts.

"In Book IV of The Republic, Plato posits rational, spirited, and appetitive aspects to the human soul." - O'Connor

Consciousness is the Key to Self-mastery

The true power that lies before our beliefs is consciousness. Consciousness grants us the power of being aware of what we absorb into the mind and what becomes part of our identity. Without this conscious act, we are exposed to our environment to either be constructed or deconstructed. As Aitchison states, our disempowering beliefs hold us back from living our full potential in life. As a child, we have no choice; that is the life we are born into. As Winn explains, children are conditioned by their nearest caregiver, and those beliefs are reinforced at school and local environments and the socialisation process.

Psychologists call this 'reinforcement perception set'. Awareness is the key to change, either physical, psychological, or emotional.

Dispenza brings this point home when he discusses the experiment with the maids. The two groups of maids are doing the same tasks, but one set is made aware that they are performing the same amount of exertion like exercise, which facilitates that group to lose weight.

The awareness of that fact brought two realities together to be realised. Gazzaniga also carried the same point home: free will is the difference between choosing or following the programme and executing the habitual task.

Is it time to change your habits?

Awareness is an interesting aspect of our reality; some may call it thinking outside the box. When an individual has the same experiences, thoughts, actions, the body's genes, and the brain's neural circuits get used to the repetition and a chronic feedback loop gets set limiting new thoughts, ideas, and actions.

Dispenza uses neuroscience to explain this stagnated phenomenon. This, in turn, is the foundation of Gazzaniga's views of having to know we have a choice. Suppose the body is programming the mind and brain, and the same events trigger the same hormones. In that case this is a restrictive loop, drastically restricting personal developments and closing opportunities before they have time to grow.

The feeling of everyday groundhog events seems to be the benchmark identifying the comfort zone that moderates our potential. This creates a familiarity between the mind, brain, and body, reinforcing the loop. Lieberman compares the H&N neurotransmitters to the comfort zone. Some individuals may tend towards the present moment, indulging in the H&N hormones shutting down the excretion of dopamine, the feel-good sensation created, regarding new activities and adventure. Like driving a car, the brakes and accelerator are not used at the same time, neither are dopamine and the H&N hormones.

Dispenza calls the absence of insidious personal trends the death of our personality; as we can then grow, we know we have a choice to think, feel and do more than we have been conditioned. Bender supports Dispenza's views by explaining neuroplasticity, the ability for the brain to grow in the areas that they are stimulated, verifying how we can adapt to our environment, which in turn cements the point of free will.

If we did live in a deterministic reality, as some philosophies suggest, would the brain have this function? From the brain to the mind, Bender refers to the subconscious and how it watches for repetition and consistency, as Holmes also confirms—making past intentions a generalisation. While some generalisations are helpful, so new information does not require a fresh view each time, they can also be restrictive and seem controlling if not put into perspective on a conscious level. Bender also confirmed with Dispenza, Holmes, Kachmann, Osho and Seligman that beliefs either construct or deconstruct our reality which is a choice if we are conscious of their intentions.

A common question that requires merit is why do negative thoughts have greater prominence in our consciousness. Perturbations are negative feelings triggered by events as Bender discusses. As our reality can be physically dangerous, perturbations are part of our defence systems and maintain self-preservation. Identifying danger is a primal duty in making perturbations seem more prominent, coupled with stress hormones. Holmes pointed out this cycle can also be exacerbated by the subconscious collecting habits and beliefs. Or, as Dispenza highlighted, due to the body's feedback system encouraging specific genes to get used to being activated.

To be conscious of our environment and how we are conditioned is half the challenge; the second part is how we internalise events once we observe them. The conscious decision to see the positive and be optimistic defines how our body reacts and what our future self will manifest into. We could say each conscious thought is paying it forward, ensuring a brighter, healthier future.

Seligman states that the opposite of conscious positive thoughts, are ones of conditioned helplessness. How we assess stressful or adverse events can compound an internal subconscious strategy that works against an individual. As Kachmann explains, whether we are aware of it or not, the autonomic nervous system goes to work producing a stress or relaxation response. This also extends to people of authority, as Kachmann clarifies.

Not doing our due diligence or being consciously aware of others, especially those we are conditioned to trust, like doctors, the media, teachers, pharmaceutical companies and practitioners, can ignite a nocebo response. Holmes also agrees with this premise and uses smoking as an example to describe how irrational habits become fixed notions and passed on from generation to generation, continuing the lies regarding nicotine.

Holmes used a simple explanation of how marketing companies used doctors to advertise certain cigarette brands in the 1940s, misusing their trust in society. Holmes explains how beliefs prohibit an individual's ability to change habits. Holmes discussed how beliefs are held in both the conscious and subconscious mind, and only when conflicts arise between such beliefs can an individual begin realignment of both parts of the mind. This internal conflict substantiates Kachmann's view that free will is a choice created from one's conscious mind.

A typical reason why clients are not successful in therapy is having sessions against their will. From a cognitive perspective, a conscious decision is required. Force is futile, and the same is observed in the most extreme situations of conditioning as seen in the war when the Chinese soldiers commandeered prisoners' liberty, the ultimate act of controlling free will.

The next is torturing that person to capitulate to the custodian's beliefs. Our mind is our sovereign, and it's our choice to change how we think and feel no matter how we are influenced. Winn explains how prisoners of war were tortured in different ways to change their views on the war and political stance. What is fascinating is that seventy percent of the nearly 8,000 soldiers that the Chinese had seemly converted to communism; only a few continued with the conditioning after the war.

Gazzaniga explains how free will is a conscious choice and compares what Winn explained from the prisoners' conditioning;

what transpires is that forcing beliefs is not effective long term. What did occur from Winn's accounts was how successful building rapport with the prisoners was to gain insights into their thoughts. The Chinese soldiers found different ways to gain the trust of the prisoners; however, when they returned to their everyday life, the majority reverted to their previous beliefs.

Toch suggested that beliefs are safe unless tested when the prisoners of war (POWs) returned home. It's quite possible the democratic environment did not support the communist conditioned beliefs to retain the new views forced by the Chinese soldiers.

Comparing what Aristotle discussed about conditioning children, it's clear from Winn's assessment of the POWs that core beliefs generated at an early age show greater stability cognitively, proving how necessary knowledge is to substantiate beliefs.

If we were to assess how many of the POWs returned home and continued the conditioning, an interesting statistic would show how many had a deterministic view when they were captive, as opposed to an internal view of being free to think as they chose instead of what they were conditioned. Excluding the fact, the POWs could have voiced ideas that were not congruent with their genuine beliefs.

Kachmann discusses the deterministic view and the consequences that lead to a change in behaviours, including aggression and an absence to help others in a state of need. Kachmann explains if our sense of responsibility is changed from a free will perspective to a deterministic view, the result is an adverse change in an individual's behaviour and observed in multiple examples, demonstrations, and tests.

Gazzaniga concurs with this observation and explains how determinism is a left-brained analytical view of reality. In his research, he witnessed determinism to encourage cheating where the influence of free will encourages individuals to show greater virtues and integrity.

Seligman equates how constraining 'conditioned helplessness' can be, and how an alternative internal strategy of 'explanatory style' brings the necessary insights into adverse events. If unattended like lost young thoughts often are, it could end up attached to an older set of opinions or beliefs and be empowering parts of our being an individual may wish to change.

Seligman, Kachmann, Gazzaniga, Holmes, Dispenza, Bender, Aitchison, and the cited authors agree on the same point. Awareness is the key. Seligman specifically indicated it is essential to identify which internal strategies an individual has gravitated towards to make the correct changes necessary after an individual is aware of unconscious conditioning.

Osho's philosophical angle confirms how communication starts to evaporate when an individual is rigid in their beliefs. Osho and Kachmann both conclude beliefs are a fixed part of one's reality that restricts growth and personal development. When such beliefs are reflected as radical, individuals may also suffer from other groups because they share the same beliefs. Our health and wellbeing are susceptible to immediate environmental changes, accessible utilities, and health care, with an additional influence that may affect our health, overly sympathising with struggling groups with the same belief system.

Osho suggests that starting any sentence with 'I am' leads to a powerful, dangerous, and committed statement of identity, which can burden individuals and restrict flowing communication with others. Dispenza agrees how conscious awareness of our beliefs can help an individual break free from old behaviours that limit our true nature.

What we ingest affects our internal homeostasis, either encouraging negative or positive feelings that influence cognitive thought processes. Perlmutter goes a step further and adds that a strong representation of reality is essential to sustain a balanced healthy mind, but what we eat is also a critical part of the process—making nutrients a key component in a healthy, stable mind and body connection.

Perlmutter directly correlated the body's inflammation and depression. He suggests the ability to remain optimistic about challenging events can be severely impaired, especially when an individual isn't aligning their nutrition with their physical and mental requirements.

Suppose inflammation is one of the precursors of depression. In that case, it's undoubtedly worth considering other feelings on the same spectrum, like melancholy, gloom, prolonged grief, and ask the question is our diet affecting our mood because of the body's inflammation response, which can either be due to the environment, chemicals or foods groups that the body may be struggling to metabolise.

A perfect place to conclude the discussion is with Lieberman's research. The examination offered is extremely relevant to the difficulties we have in this era. High sugar foods, mobile phones that carry hundreds of apps are stimulating our brains to fire dopamine more than ever seen in history, encouraging a dopaminergic world. Within the last fifty years, the manipulation of our dopamine hormones is at the neglect of our free will.

If we choose to predominantly future pace our minds in a desire for more, is that a choice or an unconscious habit? Either way, personal development starts with a choice. The competitive nature of the twenty-first century is a handicap leaving many solely focused on the next big holiday, car, or designer clothes. Industry pushes their employees to work harder; companies are compelled to increase revenue and profits for shareholders, and investors expect a higher return each year.

To carry a mobile phone and check it constantly is the same as Lieberman's rat waiting for food and getting its dopamine hit, the 'reward prediction error'. If you are, as many are, in the habit of checking your phone, this has little to do with the possible content from Instagram, Facebook, and such and highlights the 'reward prediction error'. In effect, it's a hit of dopamine that is expected from seeing a new unexpected post, article, or message that may entertain.

If looking at your phone is habitual and disturbing you in the middle of a conversation, the question is, are you in control? Can you stop when you want?

A fascinating comparison of terminology in both the rehabilitation industry and social media is the word, 'user', which is used for individuals addicted to drugs and those who use free social media platforms. I'll leave you to ponder the similarities.

Dopamine can be a distraction as it pulls our thoughts into an imaginary state which can be creative if applied correctly, as opposed to self-indulgent like an addict searching for a fix. If we believe life is about external events, what we buy, eat, be seen to enjoy, or centred around how much money we earn, the consequence is a constant trigger of the dopamine desire circuit.

Perlmutter suggests the effects of stress hormones triggered constantly creates inflammation, changing the precursor tryptophan from a fun serotonin hormone into the kynurenine pathway, which is proven to encourage depression. This conclusion highlights that our beliefs are also conditioned by our environment and an instinct deep within our psyche that ensures humanity will survive. Without a conscious observation of these instincts, these unconscious patterns can also be detrimental to our health and wellbeing.

Humanity has proven countless times, and prisons overflow with individuals who respond to situations without self-awareness, using instinct as their guide. We are responsible for living a conscious-centred life, mindful of our biases, desires, needs, and wants. Observing new tendencies, habits, and their consequences is a critical aspect of personal growth.

Without awareness, life isn't centred or balanced; we live a deterministic life guided by instinct and routine, repeating the same perception set, filtering out opportunities that we cannot comprehend.

Humanity is no doubt a creature of habit. Mankind's biochemical and neurological systems inadvertently inflict a static life. Without the conscious decision to apply free will and embrace change, we are doomed to settle for familiarity. The infamous comfort zone is the graveyard to many dead dreams and ambitions.

"Those who do not move do not feel their chains." - James Wilding

Consciousness is the Key to Self-mastery

The pursuit of happiness is a conscious choice. What has transpired from this research is that without the will to be happy or the belief that happiness is possible, an individual will leave the outcome to chance. Is it possible that happiness within some individuals occurred by accident, a perfect set of circumstances leading to an ideal outcome? Is it possible that such a set of circumstances primed for happiness leads to a sense of emptiness and search for more? The absence of awareness means familiarity may breed contempt.

Searching for more at the mercy of instinct is destructive and a conflict on the human psyche. In its innocence, the objective is to ensure humanity's survival, but the absence of understanding the true purpose of instinct is destructive in every aspect of life.

The journey through this research has given me a fresh understanding of how an individual can set about obtaining happiness and, in comparison, if a place of contentment is, in fact, a more sustainable underrated state of being.

Variables for happiness:

1. Level of consciousness
2. What beliefs support a view of happiness?
3. Refining a definition of happiness
4. Dopamine and H&N hormones firing in balance
5. Food knowledge that influences normal hormone production
6. Awareness of internal strategies inducing pessimistic states
7. The ability to search and accept help or knowledge from professionals in the above fields

No amount of positive internal dialogue will overcome a hormone imbalance of dopamine, or the 'here and now' hormones: oxytocin, serotonin, and endorphins.

The consequence of being trapped in the, 'reward prediction error' cycles is insidious in every aspect of life, relationships, past times, emotional health, education, personal development, spirituality, finances, career, health, life purpose, emotions, and nutrition.

Waiting for events to continuously supply happiness instead of actively constructing a life of purpose and meaning leaves your life to hope, chance, or superstition.

Free will and conscious-centred living are dependent on re-evaluating what psychology would describe as 'self.' Becoming the observer of who we are is one of the most liberating but discombobulating processes one can embark on.

The beginning is the most painful, as each belief creates thought, and those thoughts manifest in attitudes, and eventually, those attitudes are is displayed in our environment via actions.

The Fairy Tale of Happiness

The search for constant happiness is a fairy tale. Such myths can cause rash decisions or unbalanced behaviours and place undue pressure on yourself and others. Consistent happiness is not sustainable because it is a sequence of chemical reactions in the brain resulting from several feel-good hormones triggered when we perceive or experience an event.

To believe we should be happy all the time isn't practical or viable. A nonstop ride on dopamine isn't physically sustainable, akin to driving the car of life and constantly pressing down the dopamine accelerator, rushing past the scenery to get to a destination that is only perfect in our imagination. Indicating a slight change in the way we consider life can have a profound impact, for example, increasing awareness of daily satisfaction and contentment.

It turns out that lavishes of wholesome, energising, deliberate gratitude is more empowering than the endless search for dopamine fuelled happiness of always wanting more but not knowing how to receive from the present moment. However, the feeling of contentment is physically sustainable.

You won't feel drained or exhausted by the subtle here and now hormones of serotonin, oxytocin and endorphins, if your diet supports manufacturing. The act of assigning gratitude is where the subtle sense of contentment lies, leading to states of fulfilment and triggering the 'here and now' hormones. Everyone has something to be grateful for, even if it's as simple as a roof over their head, food on the table... blah blah blah. We have heard that statement so many times.

Let's go deeper and put some meaning into that word, 'gratitude'. Reading those suggestions of how to use gratitude, may have gone over your head, and for a simple reason. If you have the downtime to read this book, then daily food and a home are a certainty for you. We get used to our privileges very quickly, and that's why gratitude is lost easily.

You probably have a picture of your close family or friends in your home? Maybe on your living room wall, hallway or bedroom, how often have you stopped to look at those pictures and remember when they were taken, what the event was, or how those people are doing? The mind creates habits, and we walk past those pictures and mostly disregard them because the destination seems more important.

Breaking such habits is vital. Make a point to stop every so often and take a good look at those pictures. Then be present and be grateful for their health and friendship and at that moment when that energy is building within you. Choose some areas in your life that you are grateful for and that energy will go out and be received.

Building awareness is a process; you are conditioning your mind to use the quantum field to communicate and use the science of consciousness.

You are also energetically drawing more of what you are grateful for into your life. If you have an old car or one you have had for a while, sit inside it, be quiet, be present and think about all the journeys the vehicle has taken you on, all the shelter from the weather you received. Bring those feelings into the present and feel your body resonate with your thoughts. Repeat this process as many times as you need to be present and feel a genuine sense of gratitude. Practice more often if you don't feel the energy which probably means your personality is more left-brained, analytical or you are out of practice. Make it a daily habit either way.

Next time you are given a meal at home or in a restaurant, for a few moments, think about where the ingredients came from, who grew them and what they might look like, wonder how many times a day the ingredients were cared for and watered.

Wonder who processed those ingredients and imagine what they might look like, carefully picking and choosing which items will make a perfect meal, and finally, the person who cooked your dinner. The love and passion they added and the person who had spent ten hours on their feet shining you a smile making that dining experience just a bit more enjoyable. To do all of that, you have no choice but to expand your consciousness outside of yourself, which is therapeutic all on its own.

Now take a moment, take a deep breath, and directly send a quiet, sincere 'thank you' to those individuals. I promise you the more you sincerely practice this, the greater the feeling will manifest in your body. Knowing they are also in the quantum field, receiving your energy immediately as you give it, because there is no time in the quantum world. Just as a perpetually expanding sea of energy that acts as a telephone when you dial in.

If you want to take this exercise a step further, send that energy into your food, knowing you are communicating with each proton and spinning electrons to make that food even more bioavailable to your body, boosting absorption. Isn't that just magical? Unless you are eating a microwaved pizza, in that case you will probably get more nutrients from eating the box it came in!

As I was writing this paragraph, I took a moment to be grateful to share this knowledge, and I could feel myself connecting into the Oneness because I felt an automatic uplifting in my energy.

If you struggle to remember how magical life is, zoom out! We are on a rock floating through space at 66,627 mph travelling about 1.6 million miles a day! We are on a giant spaceship!

The only thing stopping the vacuum of space from pulling the air out of your body and rupturing your lungs is the invisible gravitational pull generated by the mass and acceleration of the earth. Don't get me started on how the earth was created or why the Great Pyramid of Giza has a coordinate of 29.9792458°N, which is the same as the measurement of the speed of light 299,792,458 m/s. Can that be a coincidence? I don't think so!

We can be amazed by many magical aspects of life. Stars are so far away that by the time their light travels to the earth, millions of years have gone by and they could have died long ago.

Loss reminds us to be grateful. How do you feel afterwards when you lose your car keys and it takes you hours to find them? Grateful, right? Do you feel the energy in your body then? Absolutely you do! Now you know it's a form of communication, be grateful on purpose instead of by chance.

A double-blind study with 300 college students seeking mental health counselling concluded that writing letters of gratitude significantly increased their mental health and continued for twelve weeks after the study ended.

Abnormal functions of the medial prefrontal cortex are associated with learning and decision making; however, abnormal activity is linked to depression. Using an fMRI scanner, the two groups were evaluated twelve weeks after the experiment ended. Each was asked to experience gratitude while getting scanned to examine how the brain responded. The group that had written the letters of gratitude showed greater prefrontal cortex activity than the control group.

To focus on your blessings and send out a vibration of gratefulness is the ultimate thank you to the Universe. Blessings are all around us if we choose to see them. If we don't participate in this ritual, our minds are left in comparison, living in the future, wanting, desiring, and giving back zero thanks. The secret to fully engage in the space of gratitude is how you feel as you offer your thanks; lip service doesn't apply.

Gratitude conditions our mind to be present and programmes meaningful habits which influence our character and prosperous living. Genuine gratitude amplifies your ability to manifest. Read that again.

Why Faith Healers
Don't Work in Hospitals

A fascinating observation of human behaviour is that of spontaneous physical or psychological recovery. In contrast, the medical and pharmaceutical establishments use their profound influence to diminish the support for such occurrences. Such phenomena are still observed as a natural human response through placebo and nocebo.

Faith healers in churches are often criticised for not taking their healing abilities to hospitals and get asked why they only perform on stage. This is a valid question, and from this research, the answer is clear. The intention and belief system of the individuals lying in a hospital bed is not that of an individual willing to attend a service, and stand in front of a crowd to be healed.

The powerful effects that an intention has on human biology to heal are profound. Collecting research from Dispenza, Holmes, Kachmann, and Bender has certainly compounded my insights into the mind and its capabilities. Numerous double-blind studies have documented both nocebo and placebo effects. From false knee surgery to spinal tap with no anaesthesia, the evidence of the power of belief is truly astounding. The mind-body connection is no longer a subject of the esoteric, religious, or superstitious but academic.

A fascinating conclusion that all enclosed authors arrived at was that awareness of oneself is critical to maintain and evolve into an entirely self-directed being. Without free will, evolution would be stood in its tracks, evolving at the same speed as sap dripping from a tree, with less opportunity to progress. Choosing to engage one's free will is another matter entirely but isn't that the point? To be free to choose.

Waking Up from the Matrix

The two previous subjects that society agreed to disagree on would be religion and politics, with a relatively new topic on the scene being vaccinations. Now the adage of ‹don't discuss religion or politics in public' has a new contender. These three subjects highlight how rigid individuals can get when discussing beliefs, and ultimately how our dogmatic views are slowing down the conscious evolution of humanity by simply choosing to be offended by another idea because it's not aligned with one that is subjectively set in stone, making criticism inherently threatening.

To be offended is a choice; however, the ability to compare two opposing thoughts without prejudice is a sign of intelligence. It's a growing process that encourages individuals to evaluate the opinions of others that are not aligned with their own.

When we perceive such views as a threat, the human body goes into a state of fight or flight. This reaction is driven first by the mind and swiftly followed by a dramatic increase of stress hormones changing an individual's resting state and homeostasis from a stable equilibrium of growth and repair to one of survival and instinct. Leaving indignation to be a dangerous sport indeed.

The beliefs we obtain hold a heavy weight in our life. The amount of weight on the positive side of the scale determines success and prosperity. Knowing whether there is an imbalance is to look closer to the cause; however, a simple way to gauge if beliefs are unbalanced is to evaluate your level of harmony.

Second, find the correlating beliefs that weigh the disharmonious parts of your life down, reference what knowledge supports such a belief, and conclude if those beliefs were adopted by accident or conditioned by those abusing their authority!

To fully comprehend a belief, we must understand how they are formed, whether from social conditioning, the influence of advertising, the educational system, indoctrination, or brainwashing. We should consider how we are conditioned and what, if any, the purpose and agenda of that influence.

To surrender is a choice, only if you are aware of that choice; however, most of our beliefs are programmed at an early age, and we then search to validate our reality by justifying events that validate what we already believe. This is a blind cycle, unfortunately deeming many to repeat the same behaviours in a state of trance, leaving many yet to wake up from the matrix.

To live a conscious-centred life, it is vital to observe who we have become and make a conscious decision about what we want our future self to resemble. Without a firm decision to review one's life and analyse if previous actions and behaviours correlate with new desires, limited progress is made because life is left to chance.

Significant events outside of our choice can also shape our beliefs. However, the absence of conscious direction also leaves the outcome to chance; the question is, do those events construct or deconstruct our personality and character? The only caveat in self-analysing one's nature would be not to forget we learn through our mistakes, and no one is perfect.

The Holistic View

This research highlights the vast potential for holistic therapies to influence the traditional medical field, ranging from mental health, medical procedures, and as far as bedside manner. There is a line of diligence drawn for complementary therapists governing their boundaries. However, the pharmaceutical industry deliberately excludes placebo from their trials, making the gap between conventional medicine and alternative therapy wider instead of bridging the gap.

When a change in vocabulary can influence a patient's response to pain, and a patient's diet can reduce inflammation decreasing symptoms of depression, the evidence suggests drugs are not the only answer.

The question is: What is required to make a significant change to encompass both traditional medicine and complementary therapy, to accomplish even greater success with clients and patients using little to no drugs?

"The public has a distorted view of science because children are taught in school that science is a collection of firmly established truths; in fact, science is not a collection of truths. It is a continuing exploration of mysteries." -
Freeman Dyson

Do You Have a Soul?

As an international public speaker, a favourite question I like to ask the right audience is: *Do you have a soul?*

It is interesting to observe the response, as it is not a question one answers lightly. People often need a few moments to consider the ramifications of not having a soul at all. While this is not intended to be a religious question, the highest perception in life encompasses whether God or Gods exist. Is there a higher intelligence we are unaware of, or is life simply a string of coincidences? Even an agnostic or atheist must wrestle with the facts (or the lack of them) to reside as an agnostic or atheist.

Do we have a soul? If we do, can it communicate with us, and if so, then how? You do not have to believe in any formal religion to ponder these questions and see how that feels. One of life's greatest mysteries is the idea of the soul.

Is it a metaphor? Is it a 'real' part of our being that has responsibilities? Or is the soul simply a religious or spiritual concept? I am, of course, playing devil's advocate with these questions, essentially to encourage new views and enquiries and to see if there is room for investigation.

My fascination for such questions began at an early age. As a child of about five years old, I remember pondering this question on several occasions: "If God created us, who created God"?

Looking back, I can see that there was no religious conditioning or influence in my life to offer a clear explanation for such thoughts. A large percentage of the population believe in the

Universe or a 'Higher mind'. Does that belief make it real, or is it just some kind of mass delusion? Atheists will state that there is no God, however, does that belief prove there is no Higher power or Universal mind?

Religions generally believe in some kind of 'All-knowing power' and offer their prayers in different ways, with each religion explaining their God's greatness. All religions except a couple like spiritualists and metaphysicians, by definition, require blind faith. However, I would like to suggest the following question. What if we are looking at life from the wrong perspective, and the soul is a part of our mind and is connected to our consciousness to allow us to use our physical body to sense life in this 3rd dimension?

In traditional approaches to religion, followers are asked simply to BELIEVE, with their belief based on someone else's authority. However, no matter how high the authority including books like the Bible, where is the proof?

If we refer to the soul as consciousness and let go of all the old connotations, indoctrination or misrepresentations from religion (ANY religion), would that allow for a 'fresh start' to explore new information about the soul? Would it help us to look deeper into this incredibly abstract idea from the ground up, regardless of which religion we subscribe to if any at all?

Wikipedia states that, at its simplest, consciousness is:

"Sentience or awareness of internal or external existence. Despite millennia of analyses, definitions, explanations, and debates by philosophers and scientists, consciousness remains a puzzling and controversial subject for investigation, being "at once the most familiar and most mysterious aspect of our lives."

In the following chapters, we will focus on scientific explanations and personal experiences from those of authority. Subjective and objective statements are collected from non-believers with backgrounds from a neutral or sub-neutral viewpoint, which, therefore, gives the facts (and the conclusions derived from them) greater credibility.

For many, the answer to all of life's mysteries revolves around one question: Is there a Higher power, or God, and does our soul transcend this reality into the next?

If that is so, are these forms of communication non-physical? Using a type of field much like a mobile phone uses frequencies to connect one location to another? Or is it something else?

As we examine the world of extrasensory perception (ESP), should we discredit its functions simply because we can't see or measure the 'frequency?'

Is it possible that on occasion, we experience pure coincidences? Or were they an

example of ESP and would it be considered 'rational' to think that we may have the ability to 'tune in' to a different frequency, giving us different perceptions of this reality? For example, you are thinking of a friend, and then, out of the blue, they call you, or you choose a Christmas gift, and your partner later informs you that they were looking at a similar item only a few days before.

Albert Einstein once said, "*The intuitive mind is a sacred gift, and the rational mind is a faithful servant; we have created a society that honours the servant and has forgotten the gift.*"

As you read that, think which part of your brain is used more frequently, your left hemisphere, the intellectual, analytical side working from memory and linear thinking, combining facts and logic? Or the right hemisphere, where your imagination, intuition, and creative mind resides. You may use both, but how do you know? Have you taken the time to assess your preference?

Would believing in a higher power or a collective consciousness mean we would observe more of these unique intuitive experiences, simply because we are open to them, instead of brushing them off as random events?

If you think back to the last time you bought a new car, how many of those particular cars did you see after the purchase while driving? Once your car's make and model were part of your reality, you are consciously drawn to more of the same, whereas before, it wasn't relevant to you.

The intention in asking these questions is to widen the gaze into the enigma of life, to re-examine old thoughts and beliefs, thereby freeing oneself from old dogmatic tendencies. While this research may create some cognitive dissonance (the mental discomfort that results from holding two conflicting beliefs or attitudes), the overall aim is to evolve our state of thinking and awareness. To evaluate the boundaries of what we have already conceived... even if that means taking a sledgehammer to the old foundations of beliefs (or just to know the sledgehammer is there and it's a choice).

It is essential to be an informed sceptic and actively engage the intellectual level required to look at old beliefs from a new viewpoint. Maybe the concepts in this book will push the boundaries and cause an in-depth examination of past knowledge and beliefs, hopefully providing no doubt that our consciousness is eternally evolving in this reality (and the next) and is part of a greater intelligence; whatever name you wish to give it or them.

The aim is to prove that we connect via a field of energy or consciousness as energy is stored, transmitted and received, and is open to interpretation. One of Albert Einstein's least famous quotes indeed substantiates this aim, as outlined in the following chapters:

"Everything is energy, and that's all there is to it. Match the frequency of the reality you want, and you cannot help but get that reality. It can be no other way. This is not philosophy. This is physics."

We will observe consciousness from human beings to objects, water, and plants, followed by our internal cells and the processes by which they communicate with each other, both inside and outside the body. And - the grand finale - how human beings share energetically both in this dimension and beyond for guidance in daily life.

The question is, how far down the rabbit hole do we need to go to have a firm idea of the functions of energy and consciousness, and how that energy is used as a form of communication? The study of reality starts with physics and metaphysics, which fundamentally is the core explanation of our existence.

I urge you to explore the world once again with a childlike curiosity and set aside what you think you know of this reality, all the assumptions and presumptions that generalise what you know in your world. Moreover, the world you have created and forged into a solid set of expectations and generalisations are unique to you as an individual, and when you leave this mortal coil, your world as you know it will cease to exist.

Knowing how restrictive our thinking can be, it can take a little time to re-examine the world we have created to see if it can be expanded to bring more health, wealth and prosperity to our lives.

As Frank Zappa wisely announced, *"A mind is like a parachute. It doesn't work if it is not open."*

Open your mind and allow the research provided to be as paradigm-busting for you as it was for me. As you assimilate some truly unique pioneer's knowledge, wisdom, and experience at the forefront of their research, you may define consciousness in a new liberating fashion.

The World from a
Quantum View

Before examining the idea that consciousness is separate from our physical brain, we will look a little closer at the word consciousness and its definitions. We can then dive into the world of quantum physics, biology, neurology and hydrology to help us comprehend the endless subject of consciousness and its functions. The definition from the Oxford dictionary states:

"The state of being conscious; awareness of one's existence, sensations, thoughts, surroundings, etc."

Going deeper into that definition, the height of consciousness is aware of both our inner and outer reality simultaneously. The ability to observe both states and act with the best interests of all. Consciousness, therefore, is subject to change depending on internal and external factors, such as stress, health, and the ability to perceive one's reality.

The foundation of consciousness combines all parts of our reality; being aware of the change and how we are influenced is vital to evolve our consciousness. Furthermore, our reality is in constant flux, making a lack of consciousness of self and the environment a compounding effect.

As we look at the world from the smallest scale of atoms and subatomic particles, quantum physicist Thompson Max has concluded that the world is not a solid-state but constantly vibrating, even at the smallest subatomic level. All substances and structures in the universe are made of molecules and perpetually vibrating, oscillating, and resonating energies at various frequencies, even with objects that appear stationary.

"A diatomic molecule always has some energy in the form of vibrations along an axis that connects the centre of the two atoms." - Thompson

Thompson continues to explain that once a collective's vibrational energy is a large mass, we can't measure 'quantise' vibration. For example, we view a table (composed of trillions of subatomic particles) as a whole, it is observed in a solid state.

"The energy of these vibrations is quantised, as long as the vibrational energy is not too large." - Thompson

What does that tell us about our world? What we see isn't our whole reality, and we can become closed-minded because of both our lack of knowledge and a reduction in the instinct of curiosity.

To take this concept into the real world, we live in a constantly vibrating state. Every one of us, along with all other beings and inanimate objects, are connected perpetually. We can use this information later to discuss how our minds also function in this same energy field.

Thompson also outlines how quantum mechanics has re-examined the fundamental aspects of classical physics and concludes that matter is, in fact, a wave of energy connecting everything in a field as one. Waves within the energy field that simulate the world as we know it can change into a particle when observed. Through conscious observation, waves collapse and behave as particles. *"The Copenhagen point of view does not say that a particle is accompanied by its wave function; they have no separate existences. The wave function is all there is."*

Thompson maintains that all particles are waves of energy before stationary particles. From a mass observation, it's easy to assume the opposite as that fits in with our quite literal view of the world. Max Thompson goes on to say, *"In the heart of the matter, there is an immense world, made of billions and billions of particles, which escapes our senses and intuition."*

This was witnessed first with the double slit redux experiment by Thomas Young, who first examined how light waves act when fired through a slit and landed on a screen some distance behind. He observed light and dark stripes on the screen out of the view of the slits. As the light didn't pass through the solid area surrounding the slits, the only conclusion was the light waves were bouncing off one another, enabling the light to show on the screen at a wider range than the slits would logically allow the light to reach.

Waves that bounce off each other are called interference, proving that light is, in fact, a wave. To get a firm grasp of the concept of interference, imagine a stone being thrown into a pond and imagine how the curls of small waves create ripples along the surface of the pond. Now imagine throwing two rocks into the pond at the same time, slightly apart. What you would observe is the waves colliding with each other.

The same double-slit experiment was conducted many years later, using an electronic gun that acted like a machine gun, shooting particles towards the slits. Afterwards, the marks left by those particles on the back screen were examined. Thompson describes how they found that an interference pattern would form on the screen, the same kind of interference that Thomas Young witnessed; however, when observed, the experiment's outcome changed. When the 'double slit' experiment was observed in action, the screen showed a different pattern...a pattern that resembled two lines of dots, showing no interference. *"We know that electrons are discrete particles, each with the same defined mass."*

Marianne describes this as a wave-particle duality. The act of recording the event somehow affected the experiment, changing the formation from a wave-like pattern into stripes that correlate with the slits the particles travelled through.

"The interference pattern disappears. Somehow, the very act of observing makes sure that the electrons travel like well-behaved little tennis balls."
- Marianne

Thompson continues to describe the world as we see it and how it is by stating when science reduces physical matter down to its smallest sum, it is left with space. This Quantum world is not just space and is considered to be made up of consciousness.

"Quantum physicists have discovered that within the nucleus of the atom, there is precisely a universe still unknown which they have given the name of Quantum Space or Quantum World." - Thompson

Thompson explains that the distance between the particles is essentially an illusion; we are all a single entity experiencing life in the same dimension and connected throughout consciousness. The conscious energy inside a nucleus of an atom inside one human is the same in all humans, objects, and living things. Proof of the quantum world has been observed with experiments repeated hundreds of times with simultaneous reactions. Thompson then points out how the quantum world highlights a united one consciousness or a field of energy that all matter exists inside of. One of the fascinating discoveries was the law of non-locality that operates in this space.

"That is two energy particles, despite being distant, thousands of km from each other, communicate, at the same time, in perfect consciousness. Nevertheless, the even more fascinating discovery was that the two particles

were actually... the same particle simultaneously present in different places!"
- Thompson

Dr Lipton came to the same conclusion when explaining an experiment with both an individual and a cell from his saliva. When moving the cell away from the individual and using a stress test, the cell responded in unison. The cell was then driven to the opposite side of a mountain, and the test repeated, providing the same results. The stress test and the response were recorded simultaneously. It is worth noting that neither microwave nor radio waves can penetrate that mountain, making the consciousness or the quantum world more powerful.

This experiment certainly pushes the boundaries of our reality. The next time you are thinking of a loved one or allowing your mind to enter a place of fear, remember those thoughts have effects; the energy of our mind is manipulating reality, increasing our vibrations or lowering them. Making each one of us responsible for the present moment, our thoughts, and how our future self develops or is restricted from that potential growth.

Scientific Proof of Healing Energy

We venture further from a scientific view and consider how these experiments have implications in our daily lives. We can explore Dr Bruce Lipton's scientific epiphanies to bridge that gap between life as we know it and the unseen consciousness that quantum mechanics has described.

Dr Lipton investigates how a cell's awareness of the environment is responsible for the character of a cell, not the genes or blueprint. Epigenetics, meaning ‹control above the gene', is a relatively new way to understand the science of how the cell communicates and how signals from the environment govern gene activity.

"Signal transduction science recognises that the fate and function of an organism are directly linked to its perception of the environment. In simple terms, the character of our life is based upon how we perceive it."
- Dr Lipton

Dr Lipton explains his new understanding of how the membrane functions, highlighting that the cell's brain is not the nucleus as previously presumed. The skin membrane carries receptors and receives a transmission from what quantum physics calls the field of energy. This explains how complementary medicine like acupuncture, reiki and many others work, using energy to communicate with parts of the body via each cell.

Combining the quantum physics conclusion of the field, this also explains how spiritual healing takes place.

The thought, intention, or consciousness of a healer uses the same field of energy inside each of our cells and the field between the healer and client to transmit the healing energy.

"The new science of the magical membrane, in conjunction with the principles of quantum physics, offers the simplest explanation that accounts for the science of not only allopathic medicine but also for the philosophy and practice of complementary medicine and spiritual healing as well." - Dr Lipton

Highlighting Dr Lipton's statement that consciousness is transmitted and received via a field of energy is also calculated by quantum physics. Dr Lipton explains a paranormal healing experiment by Bernard Grad, a Canadian biologist, to assess the energy field conclusion from a different physical perspective.

Grad uses plants to determine how effective a psychic healer is at transmitting energy into a beaker of water which is later used to water seeds. Grad later uses the same experiment with a depressed patient to show the opposite, resulting in the seed growth slowing down.

Demonstrating that the healer was able to influence the water positively due to their intention and mindset as the opposite response was abundantly clear from the depressed man.

"These changes demonstrated greater structural coherence of the water molecules after it was exposed to the hands of the healer and a lesser coherence when the depressed man influenced the water." - Dr Lipton

Take a moment to acknowledge that experiment and how we feel can change how effective water is at providing nutrition for a plant to grow. It's almost impossible to comprehend from an old view of the world, don't discount that experiment yet, your mind is searching for ways to make your old reality valid, your brain may be in a frantic state trying to secure your old reality or in a place of wonder and excitement.

Choose the latter for now because there are more experiments from different doctors in totally different academic fields to prove the same point about conscious energy and its functions.

How Thought
Influences Water

Dr Masaru Emoto uses crystal photographs to examine different water supplies that provide a staggering range of crystal formations, from distorted and ugly to symmetrical and beautiful, depending on many factors. Dr Emoto's research led him to investigate the influence of words on the water to find fascinating results. When placing the two words written on paper, 'thank you' and, 'fool' on two separate glasses of water and then freezing them, after taking samples of each and examining the results. Although, analytically, the results should have been the same as the water in each glass came from the same source, the words on each glass had a direct impact on how the crystal was formed.

The results from the crystals taken from the water labels with 'thank you' were symmetrical, and the opposing experiment using the derogatory word ‹fool' resulted in the crystals forming into malformed shapes.

"Water exposed to 'thank you' formed beautiful hexagonal crystals, but water exposed to the word, 'fool' produced crystals similar to the water exposed to heavy-metal music, malformed and fragmented." - Dr Emoto

Dr Emoto also evaluated the effect of the observer's consciousness concluding the results were different from the same batch of water. The only variable that wasn't consistent was the researcher's thoughts and feelings when adding the water sample to the petri dish. This phenomenon was observed on many occasions and with fifty samples per batch.

"Another important issue is the test repeatability. Many times, we have seen that crystal formation depends on the observer's consciousness." - Dr Emoto

The Power of Collective Consciousness

Dr Emoto explains how Dr Sheldrake conducts a public experiment to highlight the morphic field concept and how the consciousness of one person or a set of people is transmitted into this field of energy and received by others in their awareness. One public experiment by Dr Sheldrake on national television highlights the function of the morphic field. The experiment was conducted in three steps showing a group of people two paintings that, on first observation, looked like a random painting; however, hidden in the paintings was a woman, and hidden in the next painting was a man.

The paintings were designed in such a way as to conceal both the man and woman from the first observation. The experiment was done in three steps. First, a group was asked to observe what they saw in the painting. Second, on the television programme, the secret of the hidden people was disclosed to the group. The last part of the experiment was to use a separate group to observe the painting for the first time.

The results were quantified by more individuals from the second group noticing the man within the painting, three times faster than the first group. To create the most suitable conditions for the experiment, the viewers were restricted to England and Ireland. The results support the morphic field theory and substantiate that once one person is aware of some new information, it is then part of the collective consciousness and accessible to all.

"This experiment tells us that when someone becomes aware of something, other people also tend to become aware. It was the effect of the morphic field that led to the remarkable increase in correct responses." - Dr Emoto

Dr Emoto described another experiment by Dr Sheldrake to prove the same point. A further experiment indicated that once a pet owner decided to make their way home, the pets would simultaneously get excited before the owner entered their house. This experiment was observed using video equipment to identify the same phenomena with over two hundred examples. This research concluded the theory of telepathic communication between the owners and the pets using the morphic field to transport the intent.

"Dr. Sheldrake currently has a strong interest in the phenomena of telepathy. He conducted an experiment to find out if dogs showed a response when their masters started to head home. Using video equipment to make observations, he has been able to verify this phenomenon in more than two hundred cases." - Dr Emoto

The Negative
Power of Thoughts

To continue Dr Emoto's observations of consciousness being transmitted and received by water, he included an example in his book that a family conducted using glass jars filled with rice and water.

The experiment was constructed by identifying which thoughts and words were to be used towards each jar, with the hypothesis that negative words create negative outcomes. The two words used were, ‹thank you' and ‹fool.' Once a jar was chosen for the relevant word, it was observed for change over thirty days.

The result from the jar that was told, 'thank you,' was fermented with a pleasant smell. The jar that received the derogatory word, 'fool', started to rot and turn black. After a month, the rice that was told, ‹thank you', began to ferment with a mellow smell like that of malt, while the rice that was exposed to, 'fool,' rotted and turned black.

Dr Emoto's conclusion to his experiments is that the way we communicate influences the body's water, which is seventy percent of our body mass. Ergo the water influences how our body maintains health and a balanced state of mind to exhibit self as a fully autonomous being.

"Words are an expression of the soul. And the condition of our soul is very likely to have an enormous impact on the water that composes as much as 70 percent of our body, and this impact will in no small way affect our bodies." - Dr Emoto

Now we can comprehend how our intentions are transmitted via this sea of consciousness, quantum field of energy, or, as Dr Sheldrake suggests, the morphic field. We can communicate to water and influence the growth of a plant or influence jars of rice in water in different ways depending on our thoughts. If only we were taught this at school, how powerful our thoughts are, I can only wonder how different society would be.

Next, we will change the field of research to biology and observe further fascinating observations to support the functions of consciousness.

Consciousness is Stored and Communicated

Dr Lipton describes how each one of us is unique, and we have our own biological identity. We know of DNA, but that is just the beginning of how special we are. Each one of our cells has self-receptors called human leukocytic antigens (HLA).

Self-receptors reflect our identity, and if our organs are used in a transplant, first, a match of a minimum of the HLA self-receptors must be made, to ensure a donor body doesn't reject the organ. The greater the amount of HLA, the more likely the donor's body will accept the organ.

Each cell downloads information like a radio receives radio waves. These waves hold the information. If the radio is broken, that doesn't mean the radio waves are not being broadcasted. The information of self is broadcast and being received.

"Each cell's unique set of identifying receptors are located on the membrane's brane's outer surface, where they act as 'antennas', downloading complementary environmental signals. These identity receptors read a signal of 'self', which does not exist within the cell but comes to it from the external environment." - Dr Lipton

In simple terms, the cell doesn't only carry our identity via DNA, but it's also being transmitted to us via the quantum field. While there is evidence of this downloading of information to our self-receptors, how or why is still a mystery, or classed as 'the unknown'. The question is, are we ready to know or able to comprehend?

Dr Lipton describes a story written by Claire Sylvia. After receiving transplants, individuals can exhibit changes in their habits and tastes. Claire Sylvia was a health-conscious individual with a conservative lifestyle. Claire found after her heart transplant that she had urges to eat foods that were not part of her diet or cravings before the operation.

On investigation, Claire was informed her new heart was donated by a young motorbike rider who also had a desire for the same foods she was craving. Claire Sylvia is one of many cases reporting a transfer of habits, memories, and psychological behaviour. This new behaviour makes sense using the knowledge of human leukocytic antigens, the identity receptors 'antennas', are still part of the cell from the donor. This indicates transmission to the cell is still on, even though the cells are part of a different body because the donor is no longer alive to transmit. This leaves the only other explanation that the signal is transmitted from outside the body.n

"Supporting evidence for my belief that an individual's broadcast is still present even after death comes from transplant patients who report that along with their new organs come behavioural and psychological changes."
- Dr Lipton

Thoughts and Intent are
Transmitted and Received

I t is a common mistake to assume our thoughts don't leave our minds and that no one knows what we think. This concept is restrictive as our thoughts are transmitted into the environment and felt by others. This transmission has been proven with experiments by Dr Sheldrake, Dr Lipton, and Dr Emoto.

We are constantly influencing our reality with what we think. The following experiment concludes how intentions from groups can influence negative behaviour.

Although all human beings are connected via an energy field that's invisible to the naked eye, Dr John Hagelin, a famous quantum physicist, proposed an experiment to the Chief of Washington Police, to reduce crime by 20%.

The experiment was conducted from 7 June to 30 July 1993, and will further demonstrate the quantum field theory.

Over the two months, between 800 - 4,000 people used Transcendental Meditation, to shift the consciousness of those in the surrounding areas. This shift in consciousness was predicted to reduce crime and social stress, and improve the effectiveness of the government's daily decision making.

The experiment was carefully planned, achieving a 23.3% drop in crime, due to the meditating group and their will to achieve the objective.

"Washington crime study shows 23.3% drop in violent crime trend due to the meditating group." - Springer

Dr Hagelin's hypothesis was proven correct: When we choose to connect to the energy around us, and expand our being into the sea of consciousness or quantum field, we tap into a higher vibration of energy that can be amplified. If a group of people participates in connecting, that energy is felt by others.

The Mind is an Energy

While what we have covered so far is objective scientific research, next is more evidence of the quantum field from a subjective assessment and documented by a doctor of neurology.

Dr Jill Taylor, a neurologist who specialises in examining the brains of stroke victims, one morning woke up to go to work and experienced a severe haemorrhage in the left hemisphere of her brain. Due to her training, she was able to comprehend each stage of the event. Dr Taylor carefully defined each step to help us understand the importance of each side of our brain and how her mind was still thinking as a separate part of her physical being. However, the part of her brain that processes words was flooded with blood and essentially offline, with her motor skills and all other left-brain processes.

"It was as if the integrity of my mind/body connection had somehow become compromised." - Dr Taylor

Dr Taylor described the brain as a computer that manages data received from the external world via our senses. What we see, touch, smell, hear and taste, comprises our sensory perception. Moreover, as human beings, we experience the world from an energy level. Our senses first digest information from an energy perspective and translate that into smaller bytes of information manageable by the conscious mind to not overwhelm us.

Dr Taylor continued to explain using quantum physics how everything around us is composed of atomic particles that are constantly spinning and vibrating. If we were to see all the details at once, the amount of information entering our consciousness would be immense. We wouldn't have the conscious bandwidth to get out of bed in the morning.

What we perceive via our senses is simplified to suit the capacity of the mind, which on a conscious level is limited. The body perceives approximately one million bytes per second to the brain for processing. However, the conscious mind can only process around fifty bytes per second. Dr Taylor explained how we are immersed in a sea of electromagnetic fields and use our senses to experience our reality.

"As information processing machines, our ability to process data about the external world begins at the level of sensory perception." - Dr Taylor

After her stroke, Dr Taylor clarified what it felt like and how her awareness or consciousness expanded to a more significant proportion than her physical body. She felt like she was released from her physical body and her spirit was free to be part of the Oneness or quantum field as explained in quantum physics.

Dr Taylor was highly expressive in explaining this experience and how she felt using words like euphoria and bliss. She described how consciousness as a separate part of her being and now free from a physical form, wondered how that state of consciousness could reduce back down into a smaller space, being her physical body.

"I felt like a genie liberated from its bottle. The energy of my spirit seemed to flow like a great whale gliding through a sea of silent euphoria. Finer than the finest of pleasures we can experience as physical beings, this absence of physical boundary was one of glorious bliss." - Dr Taylor

Dr Taylor described her new conscious state as no longer a single entity but now part of everything, the energy around her as a fluid state, no more separation between two things as all is one.

"My entire self-concept shifted as I no longer perceived myself as a single, a solid, an entity with boundaries that separated me from the entities around me. I understood that at the most elementary level, I am a fluid." - Dr Taylor

As Dr Taylor reflected on her experience, she vividly remembered at one point that she was no longer able to comprehend her reality into a digestible state, and she saw her existence as it was without any lens of generalisation her reality is now one of energy, and her perception of the environment is being perceived how she feels from that energy. This was due to her left analytical brain being flooded with blood from her stroke.

"Everything in my visual world blended together, and with every pixel radiating energy, we all flowed en masse, together as one. It was impossible for me to distinguish the physical boundaries between objects because everything radiated with similar energy." - Dr Taylor

Although Dr Taylor's cognitive left brain is offline, she can still comprehend and discuss her internal dialogue. Dr Taylor compares her current state of receiving more information in the form of energy, comparing how she could engage in life as a normal human with these extra sensory perceptions. (E.S.P.)

"How on earth would I exist as a member of humanity with this heightened perception that we are each a part of it all and that the life force energy within each of us contains the power of the universe?" - Dr Taylor

Dr Taylor's left brain no longer interferes with her view of the world. She was no longer thinking on an analytical level or using her previous experience of data to project and generalise her reality. She was in the present moment and fully utilising her right brain, which is the feeling, creative and empathic side.

Her feeling right brain is fully aware without any confusion from her left brain jumping from past to future. Dr Taylor is present in the moment and connected to the energy of others. She is now utilising this heightened ability to assess her world; energy is now her brain's only way to digest her senses, and she now can estimate how much others are investing in her reality or not by feeling their energy.

"I paid very close attention to how energy dynamics affected me. I realised that some people brought me energy while others took it away." - Dr Taylor

As Dr Taylor reflected on her experience with an absence of her brain's left hemisphere, she gave us immense insight into the functions of the mind. Not the brain, because she can still remember with half of her brain not functioning. Dr Taylor explained how the right brain is connected to her higher consciousness, the Universe or Divine mind. "My right mind character is adventurous, celebrative of abundance, and socially adept. It is sensitive to nonverbal communication, empathetic, and accurately decodes emotion."

"My right mind is open to the eternal flow whereby I exist at one with the universe. It is the seat of my divine mind, the knower, the wise woman, and the observer. It is my intuition and higher consciousness." - Dr Taylor

One of Dr Taylor's conclusions was to assess the world from a new perspective. The Oneness (AKA field of energy or quantum field) and how the right brain uses the mind to connect us. Giving us the ability to create unity and support for each other, working in unison towards goals of harmony and prosperity that complement all humans and the earth. «*My right mind sees unity among all living entities, and I am hopeful that you are intimately aware of this character within yourself.*"

In trying to explain her new conclusion of life, Dr Taylor, a brain anatomist (neuroanatomist) at Harvard Medical School, summarised it by saying that her right mind is greater than she knows and that her consciousness is eternal. Dr Taylor continued to assess what we know as reality, what we sense and perceive in this world, and how consciousness is separate from physical form.

When consciousness is done experiencing via the body, her consciousness will return into the greater energy field she experienced as a reality beyond our imagination. As humanity participates with both right and left hemispheres of the brain functioning simultaneously, very few have experienced what Dr Taylor is describing. Even less, have the knowledge or skills to describe the event with the grace and elegance Dr Taylor presents. Dr Taylor's unique perspective and one from a neuroanatomist and a specialist in her field was the first to chronologically document a stroke and recover to tell the tale.

"My right mind realises that the essence of my being has eternal life. Although I may lose these cells and my ability to perceive this three-dimensional world, my energy will merely absorb back into the tranquil sea of euphoria." - Dr Taylor

Philosophy of Consciousness

Osho, a controversial religious leader and mystic, explains consciousness and intuition from a philosophical and mystical perspective.

Oxford Language describes the meaning of intuition as:

A thing that one knows or considers likely from instinctive feeling rather than conscious reasoning.

Osho makes the solid point that intuition is not scientific, but irrational. To explain intuition is to assume we can reduce it to intellect, which is impossible as intuition is beyond intellect. It's impossible to explain the cause in its entirety, because we only have ideas about where it comes from, and vague examples of its abilities. Osho goes on to explain there is a gap between intuition and intellect. Intellect can feel the intuition but knows not where it is from or its cause.

"Intuition can be felt by the intellect—it can be noted that something has happened—but it cannot be explained because explanation needs causality."
- Osho

Osho explains how intuition is of a higher realm, it's a mystical affair, and that intuition can comprehend intellect as the mind can comprehend the body, but not the other way around.

"As you go into a higher reality, the lower world of happenings has to be dropped." - Osho

There is a gap between intellect and intuition that intellect can feel. It's there but cannot be explained. The intellect knows of events that are not explainable and beyond intellect. When this is comprehended, then intellect has opened the door into the higher realm to begin to understand its magnitude. However, the strict rational intellect can also ignore the door of inner exploration and pretend it doesn't exist. Never mind opening the door into the possibility of the mysterious world of intuition.

When no intuitive experiences are comprehended, no trust can be built, leaving many questioning their faith in their intuition. This is limiting when faith is not founded on our experience but that of others.

Like all systems of trust, it's built on repetition and consistency. Once we start the journey of inner knowing and acceptance of our intuition, life transcends from physical to metaphysical to witness more of life. The alternative is to be closed off to intuitive guidance.

"Then you disallow mystery. Then you disallow intuition to speak to you."
- Osho

When we use intellect with an open mind, we are open to intuition, and intellect becomes a tool of the mind to reach higher realms of thinking. Intuition assists us in being aware of more of the same reality that was previously not on our radar.

"Then you can use reason as an instrument, and you remain open." - Osho

The conscious mind cannot reason with the concept of intuition, which intellect doesn't understand; instead, it sets a task to measure. Intuition is not a wave of light, and no measuring equipment can determine its existence, where it starts or ends.

Intellect assumes there are only two realms of possibilities. The known and unknown but there is a third, the unknowable, which the intellect cannot digest because there is no start or endpoint. Mystics refer to this realm as something that will never be comprehensible to us as humans. Intuition works from the realm of the unknowable.

"Reason can only encounter phenomena that can be divided into cause and effect. According to reason, there are two realms of existence, the known and the unknown." - Osho

Osho explains there is one single unity of consciousness, and only to understand it should we divide instinct, intellect, and intuition to go deeper into each subject. Then we comprehend each one has its purpose, complementing each other when used correctly. The human body is governed by instinct, and all-important functions are automatically dispatched. When we run, the body knows how much more air we need to increase strength or endurance within the muscles. The body knows how to simulate food and send signals when it is hungry or thirsty. This is an endless function of instinct.

Nature has created the perfect human body allowing us time to think, do, achieve and explore life, leaving our consciousness free from minimal body tasks. Animals don't need intellect and live harmoniously with the environment. The intellect is our thinking tool. It's logical and looks for meaning by assessing and calculating possibilities. Intellect creates questions to search for the answers.

Intellect is our ego, thinking more or less of who we are and creating a reality to suit our conditioned identity. This is the double-edged sword of our intellect because it gives us free will to choose and observe our behaviour if we choose. Intellect is blind and imperfect as it makes mistakes and judgments existing from prejudices.

Intuition is love, connection, inspiration, beauty, and creativity, nothing of logic or reason. Individuals who work from the heart are musicians, poets, and artists, etc. They are the minority.

"Intellect is the functioning of the head; instinct is the functioning of your body, and intuition is the functioning of your heart. And behind these three is your being, whose only quality is witnessing." - Osho

When we combine all aspects of our being, instinct, intellect, intuition, and know-how to observe and utilise these natural functions of our authentic self, we are in harmony. We are ready to explore and acknowledge self as a spiritual being living a human being existence.

"A wise person creates harmony between the head, the heart, and the body. In this harmony comes the revelation of the source of one's life, the very centre, the soul." - Osho

Instinct can let you know you are hungry, and your intuition can guide you to the ideal food for your body at the time. Intellect indicates what you usually eat from your habits, not reflecting what your body requires but what you think you desire. Instinct will make you hungry after you have eaten because you need elements that were not in that meal, and intellect will assume you have eaten and have a craving for sweet foods rather than listen to the message from the persistence of hunger.

Being stuck in intellect is restrictive; however, both instinct and intuition flow together in union. It's the intellect that breaks that union or allows it to flow. Humanity has taken instinct for granted and ignored intuition to repeat the same limited functions of consciousness. Humanity is depending on intellect too often and losing the ability to feel and know when intuition is guiding.

"And instinct and intuition function together perfectly well—one on the physical level, another on the spiritual level. The whole problem of humanity is getting stuck in the middle, in mind, in the intellect." - Osho

Intellect disrupts our consciousness with an option to consider that can be opposed to our intuition. When we go back and forth between the two, we often confuse our direction and end up in a state of being overwhelmed leading to stress. When we use intellect as an option and intuition is a powerful guide. Intellect tells us to lock the door of our car in bad neighbourhoods. Intuition tells us to carry on driving one more street.

Only after we spent hours having a window replaced do we drive past the next street, see the police station and remember that nudge to carry on driving, but recalling our intellect suggesting the next street is just as bad. This is what is called hindsight or, to the mystically inclined, not using our intuition. When the intellect is used as a transition from instinct to thought to inspiration, it's no longer a disturbance because we utilise a part of the Oneness or quantum field of energy.

"Intellect is a disturbance. But it depends on us whether we make it a disturbance or use it as a stepping-stone." - Osho

Metaphysical
Explanation of ESP

D r Masters explains how technology and research have finally caught up with the teachings of metaphysics. The scientific conclusions leave no doubt that E.S.P. (extrasensory perception), is now academic and slowly moving away from speculation. Each human being is subjected to 50-70,000 thoughts per day, leading to hundreds of emotions that turn into mental energy, connecting the mind and body. The mind can now be measured by frequency and wavelengths, with the understanding this energy is transmitted into the environment, and not only into inanimate objects, but received by other humans.

Metaphysical science works from the premise the mind is an energy and part of a field of energy receiving and transmitting. Not only to less aware frequency but to a higher frequency of which we can receive daily guidance and intuition. This energy is all-knowing, and by using meditation, an individual can raise their vibrations and connect daily to an abundance of knowledge and wisdom.

This energy is not referred to by one name in metaphysics, but several: the Universe, The Oneness, Higher mind or God. The name is not essential, as the name does not change the fact that this energy is there and ready to heal and transcend our ability to forgive. Therefore, expanding our consciousness as this higher frequency becomes a more significant part of life, teaches us the purest expression of love. "*In recent years, tests in E.S.P. and telepathy have proven what metaphysics has been teaching for years — that the energies of the mind can reach out beyond the body and make telepathic contact with people, as well as objects."* - Dr Masters

Using one of the cornerstone philosophies of metaphysics, Dr Masters explains how our mind interacts with the physical world through telepathic communication for greater prosperity in life. To cross the bridge from desires to prosperity, one must have a positive and sustainable attitude. Merely hoping, wanting and expecting an outcome is futile, no matter how many meditations or techniques one uses to bring about more prosperity.

The attitude of wanting or sending out a vibration of scarcity, is ineffective in communicating with this greater Intelligence. Not having enough is seen to be the desired outcome because that attitude is focused on not having or considering how difficult it is to receive. The Universe gives us more of what we spend time focused upon. A positive mental attitude is required to be in the flow of life and accept what is desired.

It doesn't matter if we are conscious of self-talk, limiting beliefs, and negative situations, the Universe is still co-creating. When the person manifesting is trapped in a negative cycle, they push the outcome of their new desires further away.

In metaphysics, the mind acts like a magnet, also repelling. *"When seeking love, money, success, etc., the mind will attract it telepathically, provided a positive mental attitude is maintained about the result being sought."* - Dr Masters

Following on from how we transmit our intention via our frequency; to how imperative our attitude is to cross the bridge of desire and plant our feet firmly on the ground of manifestation. Dr Masters explains the technique required to communicate with the Universe after finding a motivating and inspiring attitude. The method of manifesting is simple but easy to practise incorrectly.

Humans have a propensity to keep on persisting when their desires are not met. This sends out the wrong message to the

Universe, and it sees you wanting to be in a perpetual state of needing and not receiving. The Universe gives what we focus on the most, once a decision has been made to invite something new into our lives. The wanting can transcend towards the receiving straight away. This, in turn, activates a new heightened frequency connecting you to your future experience. You are in the field of energy telling it you have received already, on an emotional, psychological, physical level because you can feel, see, smell what it is like in your imagination.

"Programme your mind to believe and accept that what you wish to achieve is already yours." - Dr Masters

Oneness is Academic

The above chapters conclude categorically that consciousness is separate from the physical, and how consciousness is used to communicate. To grasp the concept of consciousness from the ground up, we can look at our reality from a quantum physics perspective.

We can understand the fabric of our reality, which is referred to by Dr Sheldrake, Dr Taylor, Dr Lipton, Dr Emoto, and Thomson, as the quantum field. Experiments done in different academic disciplines, including biology, neurology, genetics, and hydrology, all validate the quantum field of energy and its functions.

As we unpack these functions, two things are apparent from compiling evidence. There is a space within the smallest particles of the human body, and this same space resides outside of us. This seems to be used as a conductor or vector, as information is transmitted through this field of energy, connecting all that is within it. There is no evidence of how this is done, however, there is proof of transmitting and receiving information or consciousness from the experiments observed in the previous chapters.

Furthermore, what is categorical is the Thomas Young's double slip redux experiment. Proving that light is, in fact, a wave and not a particle as first concluded by traditional physics. When comparing the other experiments from the research, they all refer to the field of energy, morphic, quantum field, which also substantiates Thomas Young's theory.

Imagine an empty space, with no earth, people, or other planets, just space as you now know of it. Imagine a balloon in that space, the outer and inner space are the same, and that what separates the inner and outer space is a thin membrane.

The human body is made of trillions of these balloons called atoms, and so is every other material in our existence, artificial or natural. Inside each atom is the Nuclei, which is 100,000 times smaller in size. That's like putting a grain of sand inside of an Olympic size swimming pool.

We, and everything else on this planet, is more space than solid matter. Quantum physicists also describe this as the quantum world, which is still part of the unknown. What is known and observed, which Thompson refers to as an illusion, is how particles can communicate simultaneously in unison with each other, also supporting the fact that we are all in an invisible sea of energy or, as Dr Sheldrake calls it, the morphic field.

Now I want you to add a star to that space we created before, and then to lighten things up a little bit more, add in another star. Next, let's add a planet, and imagine they're all in a triangle of forty-five degrees from each other. We learn from Thomas Young that the light shining from the star is a wave, and because of interference, the light waves bounce off each other like waves in the ocean. This means that light would reach a portion of the other side of the planet, even though the stars are not positioned directly in line to the rear of that planet.

You can observe this in a dark room, with only one light source entering the room. You can observe every part of that room getting some form of light, even if it is different degrees of light and shadow than other parts of the room. Knowing the light acts like a wave highlights another observation of quantum physics: The quantum field. One could say that the field is like a sea of energy, and light uses the energy like water to create the waves. What we believe to be just air is actually a sea of conscious energy that we are all connected to inside.

What makes this space conscious, is its function to transmit our intentions and awareness from one place to another. To us, it's just air, but we and everything else in it are connected as one. This explains the experiments done by Dr Sheldrake. If we go back to the double-slit experiment, when particles are fired into the slits, the observer changes the experiment's outcome. The same was the case in Dr Emoto's water experiments: The technician's thoughts changed the crystal formations of each petri dish from the same sample of water.

Consider 50 to 70,000 trillion balloons, which coincidently is the approximate number of cells in a human body. It's not so hard now to comprehend how we are all connected to the quantum field of energy, because the same energy outside of us also resides inside us.

Each of the aforementioned authority figures uses unique scientific disciplines and methods, to measure the transmission and reception of consciousness. Dr Lipton identified how the body's cells have what he refers to as, 'self-receptors' or, 'human leukocytic antigens.' Dr Lipton uses the case study of 'Claire Sylvia,' as a clear example of this experiment after she inherited characteristics of the donor, whose organs she received. This is one of many case studies proving the functions of the H.L.A. self-receptors.

Quantum physicist, John Hagelin, conducted a social experiment to lower crime within a set timeframe, by using conscious intent. Hagelin proved a connection between those determined to send out thoughts of peace to those about to commit a crime. The substantial lowering of crime in that set period is conclusive. Dr Lipton discusses each of our cells as individuals working together as a unit, which can be said for Dr Hagelin's experiments. It was the increase in numbers of meditators towards the end of Dr Hagelin's experiment that lowered the crime rate, indicating that like-minded people in groups, do cause an effect within the quantum field, which can influence others.

The Hydrologist, Dr Masaru Emoto also witnessed - showing how the observer of the same batches of water could affect the shape of the crystals, the same as the double-slit experiment, demonstrating that the observer would change the outcome of the particle's formation. Dr Emoto's profound experiments with words that change the shape of the crystals, are a clear example of how powerful we intend to either construct or deconstruct our reality.

Comparing two unusual experiments from the opposite ends of the earth, Dr Emoto, in Japan, and Dr Sheldrake, in the USA, Dr Sheldrake uses water to compare how two individuals, a depressed man and a healer, can influence how fast a plant can grow by putting their energy into the water that fed it. Both Dr Emoto and Dr Sheldrake have proven that our intentions or consciousness can be transmitted into the water for profound results.

Dr Sheldrake goes on to verify how consciousness is transmitted simultaneously by observing pet owners and the pet's ability to receive their owners' intentions at the same moment they decide to travel home. Dr Sheldrake demonstrated the same conclusions that Dr Lipton, Dr Emoto, Claire Sylvia, Dr Hagelin and Dr Sheldrake confirmed with multiple examples. The functions of the quantum field and its ability to connect humanity as one.

Who better to illustrate how our reality is based on energy and connects all together by a field than Harvard neuroanatomist Dr Taylor and Dr Lipton. They undoubtedly bridged the gap between science and consciousness from a biological assessment, proving cells receive and transmit information. Dr Emoto and Dr Sheldrake verify water cells are designed to receive information and intentions from their environment, and change form depending on what type of intentions the water receives.

The esoteric knowledge from metaphysics is now academic and can no longer be questioned, as science has closed the gap and can demonstrate consciousness and intentions in action. Dr Taylor had the ideal training as a neuroanatomist to document her stroke and explain how the right and left brain interact. What quantum physics explained through science, Dr Taylor was able to document as a human being, to have full access to her right brain and see the world in a state of energy. Dr Taylor experienced in person what physics has been restricted to observe under a quantum microscope.

Furthermore, Dr Taylor explained what Dr Sheldrake discovered through his research, the morphic field. Connecting into that Oneness, Dr Taylor described being a single entity with all that is, as she witnessed everything in her consciousness radiated with energy.

From science, we can start to comprehend what mystics have been teaching over the ages. The intuitive guidance we once had to trust and have faith in is now proven objectively by scientific researchers and leading authorities in their chosen fields.

Although these facts have demonstrated how our intentions and consciousness use the quantum field of energy, Osho elegantly explains the third aspect. The Source, Universe, Greater Intelligence, or Higher self also uses this energy to communicate with us via our intuition. Osho explains the three aspects of our reality, the known, unknown and unknowable.

While the higher self is part of the unknowable, intuition is the steady constant that offers the most evidence in everyday life. Dr Lipton has also demonstrated one function of the unknowable as it holds information about who we are that's not part of our cells, leaving parts of our personality to be moved from one human to another after organ transplants.

Dr Sheldrake also demonstrated another function, that information is stored in the energy around us like the Cloud that can be downloaded automatically. As Osho states, intellect wants to measure to understand, yet the unknowable has no beginning or end to measure and still has functions that are observed in daily life. In addition, to move from instinct to intellect is progress; however, to evolve our thoughts and fully comprehend life, we can plug into the quantum field to utilise information and guidance beyond our comprehension. Provided that we believe that is possible.

In Dr Master's profound teachings, he speaks about the energies of the mind and how the mind can reach out beyond the body to make telepathic contact. We now know that our intentions use our energy that is also the same energy in the quantum field. Moreover, Dr Sheldrake has substantiated Dr Masters' claims in more than one experiment.

Despite not seeing this energy, Dr Masters witnessed thousands of his clients' results and how mental attitude affects one's life, making our positive mental attitude the vital ingredient in attracting what we desire. Therefore, to use this function, we send our intentions via a frequency into the quantum field to make those intentions materialise in our reality.

As Dr Masters suggests, prosperity comes from knowing how to use energy in the field. We must programme our minds to accept what is already ours, what we desire, and by connecting to the quantum field via meditation and visualisation, we can be the masters of our reality. What Dr Masters is offering is one of the secrets of life and the key to understanding the fundamental aspects of how the abstract Universe operates.

Each human being has aspirations of some kind, even if they are as noble as world peace or an example of what you would like to see more of in this world, without earthly attachments, that's still an aspiration of sorts.

To expand on Dr Masters' understanding of the Oneness that receives all our thoughts in order to manifest our abundance. What happens once the Oneness receives our thoughts cannot be explained as it's part of the unknowable as Osho would say; however, Thompson uses quantum physics to illustrate we are all in the quantum field of energy, all connected. This leads to Dr Lipton's insights and his scientific research of ‹self-receptors that receive and transmit personal information.'

Dr Masters has witnessed thousands of clients make progress using techniques like meditation, visualisations and affirmations as science catches up to prove his work's effectiveness. From Japanese Dr Emoto to American Dr Lipton. These examples are just scratching the surface of scientific experiments, that are proving consciousness and its abilities. Dr Emoto, Dr Lipton, and Dr Sheldrake all came to the same conclusion.

Our thoughts affect our reality and how we use our intent is constructing or deconstructing our health, wealth and prosperity. We can think in a Darwinian manner and be separate as a single unit, ‹survival of the fittest' and so forth; but social Darwinism has sparked many deprived causes, imperialism, racism, and eugenics, to name a few.

The conclusion from both Masaru Emoto and Dr Lipton were almost the same; humanity is constructed to complement each other; we can manifest peace on earth and contribute to each other's well-being. Dr Lipton discussed how each of our cells has their own consciousness and work in units to support the body as a whole and how society can duplicate this success.

Dr Taylor and Osho are also two sides to the same coin but, ironically, could not be two individuals in vocations further afield. Dr Taylor, a Harvard professor teaching brain anatomy, gave us a glimpse into the unknowable in her unique disability or ability, whichever way you choose to see it.

"Remembering that we are energy beings designed to perceive and translate energy into neural code may help you become more aware of your own energy dynamics and intuition." - Dr Taylor

Max Thompson, who described how the universe is constantly vibrating in a field of light, helps us understand and truly imagine what Dr Taylor subjectively described. The insights are astounding and, although her vocabulary is not the same as Dr Lipton, Dr Emoto, or Max Thomson, they were all describing the same reality but from different viewpoints.

Fortunately, there's a growing desire to prove consciousness and bring its responsibility into public view. Further research into consciousness will undoubtedly help bring the world together and replace the old Darwin theories with new examples of social and economic practices.

"Traditionally speaking, anyone who says that consciousness affects the physical world risks certain ostracisation for being unscientific. However, science has progressed to a point where the failure to understand consciousness and the mind limits our understanding of much of the world around us." - Dr Emoto.

If we are to be guided by our intuition, what would that look like, and what type of guidance would we receive? As human beings, we are under the notion that what we think about and desire in the privacy of our mind is not known by others. Our thoughts **are** transmitted, leaving antiquated notions that thoughts are private in our minds proven incorrect.

Our free will is to think what we want, but there are real-life consequences to this freedom. The experiments conducted by Dr Sheldrake and Dr Lipton proved our thoughts go beyond group dynamics or ‹group think› to telepathic communication. The saying ‹like attracts like› goes beyond a casual saying heard in new-age spiritual circles. If we are not choosing to be part of a positive frequency of this world, we may have a default mode restricting us to a repetition of negativity.

What I have observed from stepping into the minds of Dr Lipton, Dr Taylor, and the other experiments comprised, is that there is guidance from beyond, the greater intelligence, Universal mind or Higher self, which is communicating from a place of love and communion. It's a choice to be in that frequency, however, it's the one that serves us the most. To live in fear is exhausting, not sustainable, and has negative effects on the body and the water's bioavailability to nourish our being, as Dr Emoto discovered.

To live in a place of harmony and love must be the only true emotion and frequency as it's constructive and embracing, this energy without words is supportive and guiding, as Dr Hagelin learned. We can sit in the quantum field of energy with a pure heart and intention, and that alone can penetrate the minds of those who would be committing a crime. That alone indicates the power of this energy that surrounds us.

All the authors transcended their views of life to a higher realm of Oneness, and, in the end, they were surprisingly circling the same subject: The evolution of society. I was quite surprised and humbled to observe nearly all the authors ending their research similarly, but from totally different experiences and fields of study.

In some religions, it's common practice to pray before a meal, to bless the food we eat. From a quantum physics or metaphysical perspective, we don't have to be religious to send energy into food to change its structure into greater bioavailable elements. Therefore, we should be conscious of how effective our thoughts and intentions are in boosting the nutrients we eat. After digesting this information, there is now a choice to drink water or eat food and comprehend how our intentions influence the particles of nutrients we absorb; alternatively, turn a blind eye as to how a meaningful thought could increase the benefits of food and water received by our bodies.

If we embrace life from a molecular size, something magical can transpire daily as we use more gratitude and positivity in our daily lives. This state of intention can grow from what we consume of each event or situation, which deserves a moment to be thankful for, rather than just chalking them up to coincidences or random events.

Information is like a butterfly waiting to spread its wings into knowledge to take us to new heights of wisdom, transcending our intellect into intuition with each stroke of grace. If we could all experience having our left brain disabled, we wouldn't have to trust Dr Taylor in her insights and experience about the world from an energy perspective. Fortunately, other pioneers like Dr Lipton, Dr Sheldrake, and Dr Emoto scientifically prove the same concepts about consciousness and how it's used to communicate.

As a full-time professional facilitator for over a decade and a half, I have consciously observed different mental states shaped by significant events, conditioning internal representation of the world. Of course, we are all human and subject to approximately three hundred different forms of emotions, and that's normal. Fear and all that comes from fear can drive and inspire us if we choose to learn from it. However, we have a choice to move out of that state of fear as soon as possible and acknowledge if there is a secondary gain. Before we can transcend our old self, habits, phobias, fears, or negative self-beliefs, we must first become the observer of our actions.

Only then can we grow once we first acknowledge who we have become. Dr Lipton

described the two states of being, one of growth and one of survival. Both have tremendous effects from the opposite pole of attraction from loving connection and Oneness in our lives to separation, reverting to the ancient Darwinian "dog-eat-dog world of survival" as separate individuals. This research has cemented in my mind the importance of our perception in this reality and how easily our body is influenced by good health and prosperous thinking (or the opposite).

We are truly creators of our reality, and science has finally caught up to the mystical world to demonstrate consciousness. To assess the mind as the energy used by the brain is an accurate description and demonstrated throughout this book. Confirming that we have access to greater intelligence, whatever that is, is undetermined or, as Osho would say, is part of the unknowable. At least for us humans thus far.

What we do know is there is an Intelligence that Osho describes as part of the unknowable. As we move from the philosophical world to biology, human cells are designed to receive information outside themselves. When these same cells leave one body and are transplanted into another, the information is still being transmitted to the new host.

It's fascinating to comprehend how humans also influence each other and our surroundings through intention. And as that butterfly of information is about to take flight, transcending our thinking to new dimensions, remember intuition is the connection to the field of energy that will inspire, motivate and guide you.

To summarise, we all have a responsibility to be aware of our thoughts and to be

conscious of not feeding our fears. We receive intuition via the field of energy, and no matter how abstract, when we align instinct, intellect, and intuition, they all complement each other. To bring greater balance and harmony into the world, we must be the change we want to see.

By combining the wisdom solidified by metaphysics, we as human beings can incorporate a higher dimension of awareness, and manifest from both a human and spiritual perspective. Once we learn to step between these worlds of awareness, the ability to live in prosperity can happen effortlessly.

The Ten Functions of the Quantum Field Proving Consciousness is Interactive

To recap, we have covered many unique experiments concluding different functions of the quantum field that surrounds each of us:

1. **The quantum field knows when it is observed** - Light is a wave function

2. **Positive vibrations influence the quantum field to affect physical matter** - Intention and human frequency change the bioavailability of water

3. **Our experiences are recorded into the collective consciousness to be accessed at will** - collective consciousness stores and transmits knowledge

4. **Thought alone is powerful enough to connect, simultaneously, regardless of distance** - Dr Sheldrake's pet experiment demonstrates connecting consciousness between a pet and its owner is immediate

5. **There is a Higher intelligence that receives and transmits data** - Dr Lipton substantiates the self-receptors "antennas" receiving data from the quantum field, giving new personal preferences to transplant patients

6. **Positive vibrations are amplified when connected to the quantum field.** John Hagelin demonstrates group vibrations transmitted to the quantum field, lowering crime in the local vicinity by 23%

7. The quantum field uses energy to communicate, not words, confirming E.S.P

8. Intuition is the voice of the quantum field

9. The quantum field is used by a higher intelligence that responds to our intentions

10. The 3d reality is designed to manifest through desire, focused attention and intent

We no longer require faith in someone else's miracles; living a life using these functions is living on purpose, not by chance. We are the second half of the divine experience; that is your responsibility. Is it time to be aware of your thoughts and vibrations, knowing a higher awareness is receiving them? This intelligence has the power to influence reality beyond our ability to comprehend and now we have proof of its existence.

It was my pleasure to share my career and educational conclusions through thoughts, stories, and research of some of the highest regarded experts in their field. I trust this information will inspire you to help yourself and others effectively in the shortest amount of time possible because people deserve that. I trust my teachings about the mind combined with practical but straightforward metaphysical techniques will encourage you to learn further about the subconscious mind to live your most prosperous life.

If you take one lesson away from this book, learn how your inner and outer awareness, also known as consciousness, can drastically change your life for the better.

If you have a level of awareness to notice what you have been conditioned into, you can change and evolve. It's that simple, no awareness = living a conditioned life. Is it time to reinvent yourself?

Don't be afraid of change; embrace it because life around you will change with or without your consent. Adapting is to surf the wave of destiny, or the alternative is to get crushed by the weight of the waves. The waves teach us lessons either way. We are living in a sea of consciousness; the waves are inevitable. Some wise words from the famous pirate Captain Jack Sparrow — "*The problem* is not *the problem*. *The problem* is your attitude about *the problem*." Sparrow may not have considered a serotonin imbalance due to a restricted diet with his rum philosophy, but he was halfway there.

"Mistakes are the portal of discovery." – James Joyce

Live a life of high vibration. What you let into your mind and body has energy; choose the high vibrating forms of food and thoughts. It's not possible all the time, and the lower vibration serves humanity, too. If we were only to taste the sweetness of life, how would we truly know what the sweet nectar of life has to offer? If it wasn't for the bitterness.

The poles of attraction are necessary. No love without hate. No peace without war, no creation without destruction. Change is how the Universe creates balance. Without extreme emotion, hatred, jealousy, fear, anger, and control, how would we grow and evolve into a place of greater love and all that comes from love, freedom, joy, happiness, forgiveness and compassion, etc.? Find meaning in your suffering and transcend it. And as the philosopher Rumi once said, "Sorrow prepares you for joy."

Forgive yourself, as that act will teach you to forgive others faster. When you see parts of your darker nature for the first time, it's challenging, overwhelming and feels unnecessary. Some would describe it as painful. The sooner you use philosophy to comprehend the lessons, the quicker you can overcome them; when you forgive, you heal.

Holding onto resentment, anger, hatred, and self-pity due to other people's actions is like drinking poison and expecting someone else to die. Trying to reason with life is pointless;

to attempt to bargain or live in denial creates needless circles of repetition, that can lead to feelings such as anger, stress, anxiety, depression, etc. As Kübler-Ross, a renowned psychiatrist suggested, our aim is to move forward to acceptance.

The ego-mind wants to understand life. However, many parts of life are not comprehendible. Life creates lessons to move through and reflect on with strength and wisdom. The 'why' is useless when attempting to find a reason for adversity in life. The 'why' traps the ego-mind and causes circles, a maze without an end. Asking the pointless question of, "Why did that happen to me?", can be replaced with, "What can I learn from that?" Taking responsibility is empowering and searching for external blame is disabling.

If you subscribe as a co-creator or spiritual being, don't jump the proverbial fence when it serves your ego-mind. You are a spiritual being living an incarnated experience. Using philosophical explanations trumps analytical reasoning every time because the human outlook of life has a minuscule range of comprehension.

Discover how to transcend intellect to intuition because the Source, Universe, the Almighty, the Higher mind, God, or whichever name you wish to assign, is waiting to direct and inspire you. You are a spiritual being living a human experience. Free yourself from such words of death and actively replace them with transcending or simply going home.

Mourning the death of a loved one suggests you can no longer hear, see or communicate with them. The energy of the soul is eternal. When we transcend these antiquated beliefs about death, we can dramatically shorten the mourning process and celebrate life, focusing on what we received instead of what we have lost.

Living a spiritual life means having a divine connection with a unique meaning and philosophy. The act of connecting comes with a responsibility. It requires much deliberation and perpetual reflection. Otherwise, it's not a spiritual practice, it's just a stagnant idea. Like many religions, beliefs are literally fixed in stone, not debatable or to be questioned, but blindly followed, requiring hope and faith. This is for the simple reason that an idea has remained the same for a long time, somehow means it cannot be questioned, because too many new ideas would change the meaning of the ‹book› that religion is based upon.

Learn how to effectively use gratitude as a daily skill, knowing that you are directly communicating with the Oneness to prove you are in tune and aware of the magic of life. The simplest meaning of Magic is a desire made real.

If you feel depressed, low, or have anxiety, I can categorically suggest you have drifted into yourself away from the Oneness. You have become an isolated unit of one, appose to part of the collective Oneness. Remember to pick up the quantum telephone to say 'thank you' through the energy of gratitude. The action of raising your vibration connects you to the Oneness.

The Universe doesn't speak a language, it speaks frequency. You cannot be within yourself and send the energy of your intentions out at the same time.

To make fast, safe, lasting change, utilise the power of the subconscious mind. How often do you use your subconscious mind on purpose? The subconscious mind is hundreds of thousands of times more powerful than your conscious mind. By the time you are eight years old, your subconscious has recorded up to 10,000 words, and by the time you are an adult, between 20 and 35,000 words. Ponder on that for a moment, the brilliance. Your unfair advantage is within you, the edge you have been looking for.

I bet you a cappuccino that I can make your subconscious mind respond to some simple statements I write here. If you agree, I'm going to hold you to my coffee, is that fair? I like to trust people; life is so much simpler that way. Why waste time judging when everyone shows their actual colours? In the end, that's human nature.

Okay, here we go...

Hold out your hand and imagine you have a sweet in your palm.

Do you remember those ones that glisten with sugar coating, crunchy and soft in the centre but super sour?

Just imagine one of those, see its size, and I bet you can remember the smell; they almost smelled sour, do you remember?

Now you know what's going to happen when you put it in your mouth, right?

You won't be able to stop sucking on that burst of tart flavour because it's so good.

And you want it to last forever. But you simultaneously want to bite into it and let all those joyful flavours swish around your mouth, don't you?

Now imagine putting that very sweet in your mouth and remember that sensation.

Are you salivating? Of course, because your imagination was activated.

Imagine all the hidden resources in your subconscious mind that just need a little vision and intent to access for greater health, wealth and prosperity in your life; powerful, isn't it?

Go within or go without. Go within yourself and explore the vast landscape of your conscious, subconscious and super subconscious mind or the quantum field.

Or live in ignorance of this inner reality that ironically shapes our outer world regardless of our acknowledgement.

The Power of Change Lies in Subconscious Realignment

Milton Ericson, a famous psychologist, articulates subconscious realignment accurately:

"Patients are patients because they are out of rapport with their own unconscious. Patients are people who have had too much programming – so much outside programming that they have lost touch with their inner selves."

The programming can also be from an excessive internal dialogue, finding a conclusion that works against your authentic self.

Many years ago, I had a client, Wendy, who was going through a state of feeling unsettled in her life; she had a conflict but no idea where it was coming from. Wendy was an accomplished lawyer in Hawaii and worked to create her ideal life, exercised regularly, had a balanced diet and work-life balance, but something was not feeling right. Her subconscious mind was communicating with her, but she couldn't place the message.

After half an hour of conscious digging and getting nowhere, I asked if Wendy was open to communicating directly with her subconscious mind, as that is where the message is from.

Upon agreeing, I assisted her into an altered state of awareness. I used a simple metaphor to communicate (the subconscious mind loves metaphors, that's why we have visual dreams, as dreams are also a form of communication). When the session was finished and Wendy was back in full waking consciousness, I asked her what she found in the metaphor that she had previously forgotten.

She sat across from me, looking down at the floor, silent and still; she then suddenly looked over and said, "A wedding ring." I was confused as I didn't know she was married. I inquired as to how that is relevant, and she smiled. She said in a clear voice, "I understand now."

She then continued to explain she was married for many years, and towards the end and including the divorce, it was a little traumatic and took a while to get over. Wendy said her boyfriend is suggesting they move in together, and she now understands what the feeling is about. Although the new relationship is rewarding, her last relationship ended badly, leaving a lasting impression. Wendy's conscious and subconscious mind were not aligned; her current desires and previous programming conflicted.

After the session, Wendy was now able to negotiate with her feelings, Wendy felt in control, so I didn't hear from her again, which is a good sign in my line of work.

Phobias, irrational fears or limiting beliefs, are all programmes in the subconscious mind causing conflict, not aligned with the conscious mind. While I have the utmost respect for traditional therapy, rarely do they use the power of the subconscious mind to find fast, safe relief for patients. I'm not sure if the treatment's speed leaves the impression that fast recovery reduces their income or it's a lack of knowledge of the subconscious mind.

When fast recovery is what people are amazed by, people cannot help themselves but talk about amazing experiences. Word of mouth is always the best form of marketing, and on countless occasions, new clients have flown from the other side of the world because of recommendations. Leaving the benefits to one session resolutions outweighing longer processes, when they are suitable of course.

Stages of Learning

I suggest reading Mind-Bending Beliefs a few times, and I can promise you this, you will notice more each time if you have applied what you learned from this book from the previous read. Information isn't knowledge; we must experience the information and make it our own to be wiser.

We all go through stages of learning:

First stage; you will be **unconsciously incompetent**; you don't know how bad you are at applying your new skills. To sit in the Oneness or observe life from a quantum perspective takes practice.

Second stage; you will become **consciously incompetent**; you now know how bad you are at applying your new skills.

Third stage: you will become **consciously competent,** and your life will be full of symbols and guidance as you notice what was once perceived as coincidence. You use many functions of the quantum field, and the Universe responds with each moment you send thanks via your gratitude.

Fourth stage: unconsciously competent. You have made the quantum functions part of your life and use them without thought. You know you are connected and transmitting and receiving from the Source for daily direction and inspiration to live as your authentic self. You still make mistakes as consciousness is fluid and subject to a variety of internal and external influences, and that knowledge itself evolves your thinking and ability to evolve.

This process of conscious awareness explains why each time you read Mind-Bending Belief's you will take a little bit more each time to apply; working towards the magical life you deserve.

Subconscious Realignment Program

Do you have a first aid box for your mind?

Isn't it strange how we're not taught how to use our consciousness?

What techniques do you have to move your mind away from depression, anxiety or states of being overwhelmed? What strategy do you use to prevent those experiences?

Some people have a natural ability to manage their emotions effectively. They may have an ambition and drive to achieve effortlessly, all by chance, because no one gave them a manual either.

For the rest of us mortal humans, we make so many mistakes, and some leave a lasting impression on our mental state, which increases our fears and vulnerabilities.

When falling into a rut of stress, depression or anxiety, do you leave to chance the time it takes to cycle out of this state?

Or do you have another strategy to reset yourself quickly to maintain balance?

There is a potential gap between not managing our thoughts, feelings, and actions, but still being a fully functioning member of society, and needing traditional help with a psychologist or counsellor.

That glorious gap in the middle can be filled with personal development. When we learn how our mind works, we find clarity and direction much faster. When we fall into spiralling states of negativity, stress or anxiety, we have the skills to realign ourselves.

This gap is a huge opportunity for potential growth. When noticed, the journey to become the best version of ourselves, starts. We increase our prosperity, aim our focus, and achieve contentment.

Bear in mind, this opportunity to tap into how the mind really works and how we receive the best from life, is an optional extra. No one is going to pressure us to become the best we can be, or to surpass the societal expectation of doing the bare minimum.

It is a choice. It's our choice. Your choice.

Unfortunately, searching for help can feel uncomfortable. We can put our lives in the hands of the wrong people, by seeking advice from friends with their own personal bias. Your intuition is your best advisor. How many times have you kicked yourself in hindsight for not following it? On reflection, you knew the best course of action, but your analytical thinking navigated you in another direction.

Is it time to change that?

Are you fed up with your current methods of processing and problem solving, receiving the same dissatisfactory results?

Subconscious Realignment has two fundamental concepts:

- To let go of the past, freeing up the ability to make conscious decisions that are aligned with the authentic self, rather than the conditioned self.

- To connect to the Oneness, using intuition as our internal guidance system, to live a life of purpose and fulfilment.

There are powerful but simple techniques that, once learned, complement your daily life. After years of observing clients with common symptoms, often due to a lack of knowledge, I decided to develop the **Subconscious Realignment** Programme to equip everyone with the tools to become self-sufficient, and to empower others with an increased level of intuition.

Ready to boost your state of mind?

- Feel more confident in your thoughts and direction
- Discover your authentic self as you let go of your conditioning
- Improve motivation and success
- Identify a positive self-image for deeper self-love
- Boost your focus and determination
- Learn the secret to overcoming procrastination
- Reinforce your mind for future challenges
- Learn how to negotiate with yourself and win every time for greater health, wealth and prosperity

Pressure is a natural, intermittent response that drives us forward, giving us that push we need in order to act. When that push is constant and no longer periodic, those same helping hormones can hinder, causing acute symptoms to the body and mind. Suppose the acute phase progresses gradually into a chronic phase from days, to weeks and months.

You may not realise how your actions have adjusted as a response to those same thoughts and hormones that were helpful in the beginning. All that started with a state of mind and a lack of knowledge of how the mind works.

Imagine sitting in a car and having to guess how to start it. That's the experience of every adult when learning how the mind works, and for some of us, it takes time before getting it right.

Use the link below to start your free trial.

For more info, to go **www.anthonyaugustine.co.uk/SR**

Subconscious Realignment Practitioner Training (SRPT)

Do you have an interest in helping others? Or perhaps you have a natural inclination but get caught in co-dependent situations, or the results you get are not what you intended? In such cases, some professional training would certainly help.

If you are a practitioner, you can take your practice to the next level by incorporating your skills with powerful subconscious realignment techniques. Learning how to manage your client's subconscious mind will boost the effectiveness of your current skills, because every one of your clients has a subconscious mind.

For more advice, join our free workshop to discover how subconscious realignment techniques can assist your practice, or help you to start a new and rewarding career.

Use the link below and redeem your free workshop today.

www.anthonyaugustine.co.uk/srpt

*"Thank you for letting me lend my light to yours.
Together we shall shrink the darkness until there is only
light."*
- The Professor and the Madman

Glossary

These brief explanations are no substitute for in-depth enquiry

Acidosis
Acidosis is a common condition when the body's balance of alkaline minerals is depleted or low, causing symptoms; increased weight, low energy, acid indigestion and, in some acute cases, leading to severe disease or illness.

Affirmations
Positive affirmations are internal statements repeated to increase a positive mind and vibration.

Anaesthetic
An anaesthetic is a drug that produces a complete or partial loss of feeling.

Analytical
The process of relating to details of facts or information or careful, systematic study.

Subatomic Particles
There are three types of subatomic particles: protons, neutrons and electrons—the fundamental components of all matter.

Autonomic Nervous System
The autonomic nervous system is the part of the peripheral nervous system responsible for regulating automatic body functions, such as your heartbeat, blood pressure, digestion and

breathing. The autonomic nervous system automatically governs a range of body processes without conscious effort.

Autonomous Being
To live life according to one's own reasons and not be the product of manipulative or external influence, to be independent.

Bioavailability
The ability of a drug or other substance to be absorbed and used by the body effectively.

Biological
Something that relates to life or living organisms.

Co-Creator
Accepting humanity is the second half of the divine experience to be the master of reality and prosperity.

Cognitive
Cognition is a term referring to the mental activities involved in obtaining knowledge and comprehension.

Collective Consciousness
A collective memory that all beings share, connecting energy and information.

Complementary and Alternative Therapy
Treatments that fall outside of mainstream healthcare.

Complex Compulsive Habits
Compulsions are mental acts or repetitive behaviours that an individual feels compelled to perform in response to an obsession. When a compulsion has many supporting beliefs and triggers, it is classed as a complex compulsive habit.

Dimensions

The physical world as we know it has three dimensions of space which are length, width and depth and one dimension of time, encompassing the mind, body, the external world.

The Fourth dimension is the inner realm, higher consciousness, that many only access in a dream state via the astral or etheric plane. According to string theory, the universe operates with ten dimensions.

Most humans, being three-dimensional organisms, cannot YET consciously sense or perceive higher dimensions. Lower and higher dimensions can also be referred to as levels of vibration. Neither can be judged as better or worse, only closer to the Oneness of all that is or further apart. All denominations occupy the same space and time, transitioning from one level to the next, depending on conscious awareness.

Consciousness

A state of inner and outer awareness, a fluid state of being that expands and contracts from the Oneness depending on external and internal influences.

Darwinian

A theory suggests that organisms with the strongest and most desirable characteristics are best able to survive and reproduce.

Determinism

A philosophy that suggests all events, including moral choices, are entirely determined by previously existing causes—the opposite of free will.

Dopamine

Dopamine is a type of neurotransmitter. Made by the body, your nervous system uses it to send messages between nerve cells. AKA the molecule of more, dopamine is an elating hormone excreted when the mind is focused on pleasurable future events and when certain nutrients are ingested.

Ego
An individual's sense of self-esteem or self-importance.

Elaters
The subconscious mind projects positive emotions into the consciousness as a response to perception.

Electromagnetic
The passage of an electric current develops magnetism.

Emotional Freedom Technique
An alternative treatment for physical pain and emotional distress.

Emotional Triggers
An intense emotional reaction.

Empathic
Empathy is the capacity to understand or feel the experiencing of another from within their frame of reference—the ability to place oneself in another individual's situation.

Esoteric
The knowledge that's intended for or likely to be understood by only a small number of individuals or groups with specialised interests.

Epigenetics
Epigenetics is the study of biology focused on changes in gene function that are heritable and not attributed to changes in the D.N.A. sequence.

Essential Amino Acids
The body cannot make essential amino acids. Amino acids are molecules that combine to form proteins.

Extra Sensory Perceptions
AKA, the sixth sense, a perception that occurs independently of the known sensory processes. It uses the quantum field to collect information sensed by the mind.

Extroverts
Extroversion is characterized by sociability, talkativeness and assertiveness.

E.E.G.
An Electroencephalography (E.E.G.) is a test that detects abnormalities in your brain waves.

fMRI Scanner
An fMRI scan is a functional magnetic resonance imaging scan that measures and maps the brain's activity.

H&N Hormones
Serotonin, oxytocin, and endorphins hormones, also known as endocannabinoids.

Haemorrhage
Blood loss.

Harmonisers
Empowering subconscious emotions.

Homeostasis
In biology, homeostasis is the state of steady internal, physical, and chemical conditions maintained by living systems.

Human Leukocytic Antigens (H.L.A.) AKA Self-Receptors
Human Leukocytic Antigens reflect identity in two ways. First, the cell carries our identity via D.N.A. and receives and transmits the cell's identity via the quantum field.

Hydrology
A type of science that studies water.

Hypothalamus
The hypothalamus is an area of the brain that produces hormones to maintain the body's internal functions and balance.

Learned Helplessness
A behaviour pattern and the collapse of problem-solving strategies when obstacles arise.

Internal Representation
The internal representations that an individual can make consist of pictures, sounds, feelings, tastes, smells, and self-talk to simulate their unique view of the world.

Introverts
Introversion is a significant personality trait. An individual who feels more comfortable focusing on their inner thoughts and ideas rather than what's happening externally. Is prone to get overwhelmed by excess external sensation.

Intuition
The natural knowing capacity. Inner knowing; the immediate apprehension of truth without the use of intellect.

Kynurenine Pathway
In the central nervous system (C.N.S.), the kynurenine pathway starts with the conversion of tryptophan into kynurenine. The kynurenine pathway has received increased attention due to its connection to inflammation and depression.

Mesolimbic Pathway
The mesolimbic pathway is also referred to as the reward pathway, as it is one of the central dopamine pathways of the brain.

Metabolize
The human body or an organ processes a substance to extract its nutrients by metabolism. The three main reasons are for creating energy, extracting building blocks, or eliminating metabolic wastes to sustain life.

Metaphor
A metaphor is a figure of speech in which a word or phrase denoting one kind of object or idea is used in place of another to suggest a likeness or analogy between them. A metaphor can be used to make a comparison between two things that aren't alike but do have something in common.

Metaphysics
Metaphysics is the branch of philosophy that examines the abstract causes of things, space and time, causality, necessity and possibility. Metaphysics includes ideas about the nature of consciousness and the relationship between mind and matter.

Microorganisms
A microscopic organism, particularly a bacterium, virus, or fungus.

Modelling
The process of demonstrating a pattern of specific skills that results in excellence.

Morphic Field
The morphic field is an energy field that surrounds the entire biology of all living beings that is scientifically proven to receive, store and transmit information via energy.

Mystical
Spiritual meaning or reality that is not obvious to the senses or the intellect.

Naturopath
Naturopaths aim to prevent illness through stress reduction and changes to diet and lifestyle—a form of alternative medicine.

Nerve Impulses
An electrical charge that travels along the membrane of a neuron. It is how a nerve cell communicates with another cell.

Neural Circuits
The pathway in the brain for thought and movement.

Neuroanatomist
The study of the structure and organization of the nervous system.

Neurology
Neurology is the branch of medicine involved with the study and treatment of disorders of the nervous system.

Neuropeptide
Neuropeptides are the most abundant chemical messengers in the brain and play a role, particularly when the nervous system is challenged by injury, pain, or stress.

Neuroplasticity
The brain's ability to reorganize itself by forming new neural connections throughout life, compensating for injury, disease and adjusting activities in response to new situations, adapting to change.

Neurotransmitters
Chemical messengers in the body carry, boost, and balance signals between neurons. Examples of Neurotransmitters are dopamine, glutamate, serotonin, norepinephrine and gamma-aminobutyric acid (GABA).

Nocebo
Latin for 'I shall harm'. The nocebo effect is the opposite of the placebo effect. Nocebo effects are adverse events produced by negative expectations.

Obsessive-Compulsive Disorder
Obsessive-compulsive disorder (O.C.D.) is a mental health condition with obsessive thoughts and compulsive behaviours.

Oneness
Oneness is an experience that transcends the mind and body, connecting to all that is, was and will ever be. As we recognize higher dimensions, we are all manifestations of the same energy. We are all One experiencing life at different stages of awareness with amnesia of our true origin and potential.

The experience of Oneness from a spiritual perspective is best portrayed as the union between the two energies of self and the Universe or Creator. Oneness has been documented for centuries throughout Eastern and Western religions, philosophies and Mystics, and is now confirmed with different types of science and multiple experiments.

Oxytocin
Oxytocin is a neuropeptide produced in the hypothalamus excreted to increase the repair of the body, reduce pain and decrease inflammation. Commonly known as a bonding hormone, and excreted as a result of human contact creating a present warm feeling.

Perturbations
Negative emotions are projected from the subconscious mind as a warning system for dangers in the environment. Perturbations have the highest authority and are connected to the primal instance of survival. Awareness and negotiation of perturbations are essential to living a conscious-centred life.

Pessimistic

Pessimism is a negative mental attitude when anticipating an unwanted outcome from experience.

Placebo

A placebo is a substance or treatment that encourages the body to repair. A psychological phenomenon that creates rapid positive change within the brain and body through thought alone.

Phobia

A phobia is an irrational fear projected from the subconscious mind leading to behavioural symptoms. From the Greek word Phobos, which means fear or horror.

Precursor

A substance from which another is formed; e.g., serotonin is the precursor to melatonin to induce sleep. One of the reasons individuals under high stress struggle to sleep.

Prefrontal Cortex

The cerebral cortex covers the front part of the frontal lobe of the brain. Responsible for moderating social behaviour, decision making and personal expression.

Probiotics

Probiotics are live microorganisms that improve or restore the gut flora, a complex ecological system which is 40 trillion bacteria strong. Two of the most important roles have to do with immune system protection and metabolism and are responsible for 80% of the body's serotonin production.

Psyche

The psyche is the totality of the human mind, conscious and subconscious.

Psychosomatic
A physical illness or other symptoms caused or provoked by a negative mental attitude, internal conflict or stress. Transferring energy from the mind to the body.

Quantum Physics
Quantum physics is the study of matter and energy at its most fundamental level that explains our physical reality at the scale of atoms and a subatomic scale.

Receptor Site
Receptor sites are proteins that can recognise and bind to specific molecules. Receptor sites act as a lock for hormone keys.

Reiki
Reiki is a Japanese form of energy healing.

Reinforcement Perception Set
A reinforcement perception set is a tendency to view life from a firm set of beliefs, values or standards conditioned by the environment. They influence an individual's expectations, motives, and interests from a particular frame of reference.

Reward Prediction Error
Reward prediction errors involve the difference between what you expect and what you get that influences dopamine excretion.

Ritalin
A stimulant drug which is used to treat attention deficit/ hyperactivity disorder and narcolepsy.

Secondary Gain
Secondary gain is an external motivator, a subconscious action to receive attention or relief. Secondary gain can manifest as disability, illness or disease.

Self-Fulfilling Prophecy
A self-fulfilling prophecy is a process of an individual's expectations manifesting in their reality. Thoughts send out a frequency into the morphic field to match experience with the anticipations. From a subconscious perspective, the repetition of thoughts conditions the subconscious mind, which goes to work aligning your desires with your reality.

Serotonin
Serotonin is a hormone that stabilizes mood and increases feelings of well-being and contentment. Within the pineal gland, serotonin is converted into melatonin and has long been associated with controlling the sleep-wake cycle.

Signal Transduction Science
Using small molecules, cells talk to each other. Specific cells have individual receptors, which can activate different pathways upon receiving a signal. For instance, to help regulate glucose in the blood, insulin can cause muscle cells to uptake and store glucose, triggering liver cells to stop creating glucose.

Skin Membrane
There are four types of membranes in the body. They are thin layers of tissue
usually connected to an underlying layer of connective tissue.

Subconscious
The more significant portion of the mind that holds your identity: beliefs, values, memories, standards, morals and, in its entirety, uses experience to simulate your character and personality. It is the hard drive instead of the conscious mind, which is more like a desktop of a computer, limited in its functions and only utilizes programs when required. The subconscious communicates with feelings, symbols and metaphors.

Subconscious Realignment

Realignment is required when internal conflict is caused by contrasting beliefs between the conscious and subconscious mind causing symptoms in daily life. The magnitude of the symptoms reflects the contrast of the beliefs.

Super Subconscious

Imagine the subconscious hard drive of your mind being connected to the internet, into the Oneness.

Tryptophan

An essential amino acid; your body cannot produce it. Tryptophan is necessary for making proteins. It is naturally found in red meat, poultry, eggs, and dairy. Tryptophan is the precursor of serotonin.

Vector

A quantity or phenomenon is determined by its position from one point in space and relative to another, having direction and magnitude. Examples of vectors in nature are velocity, weight, momentum, force, and electromagnetic fields.

Works Cited

Aitchison, Steven. *The Belief Principle: 7 Beliefs That Will Transform your Life. CC.Y.T. Media LL.T.D.*2020. Printed

Attitude.co.uk/article/hugh-jackman-almost-gave-up-his-dream-after-his-brother-called-him-a-sissy/17681/ 2018-04-25 Web

Aristotle, The Philosophy of Aristotle; Goodreads.com/quotes/709859-give-me-a-child-until-he-is-7-and-I 29.4.2021 Web

Bender, Sheila Sidney, Ph.D., and Sise, Mary T., LL.C.S *The Energy of Belief* Elite Books 2007 Printed

Dispenza, Joe. *You Are the Placebo* Hay House. 2014. Printed

Gazzaniga, Michael. *Who's in Charge?* Free Will and the Science of the Brain Little, Brown Book Group. 2011.Printed

Holmes, Christopher. *The Biggest Medical Mistake of the 20th Century (Nicotine: The Drug That Never Was Book 1).* Chris Holmes. 2007 E-book

James wilding blog/2013/02/20/those-who-do-not-move-do-not-notice-their-chains-rosa-luxemburg 29.4.2021 Web

Kachmann MD, Dr. Rucy. *Nocebo: Placebo's Evil Twin.* Self-published (no year) E-book

Lieberman, Daniel Z.; Long, Michael E. *The Molecule of More* BenBella Books, Inc. 2003. Print

Osho. *Intuition (Osho Insights for a New Way of Living)* St. Martin's Publishing Group. 2011. Printed

O'Connor, Timothy plato.stanford.edu/entries/freewill/ *Mon 7th January 2002* Web

Perlmutter, David. *Brain Wash Detox Your Mind for Clearer Thinking, Deeper Relationships and Lasting Happiness* Hodder & Stoughton. 2020. Print

Seligman, Martin. *Learned Optimism: How to Change Your Mind and Your Life.* John Murray Press. 1991. Print

Toch, Hans. *The Social Psychology of Social Movements* (Psychology Revivals) Taylor and Francis. 1966. Printed

Winn, Denise. *The Manipulated Mind.* Malor Books. 1983 E-book

Steve Silberman/ wired.co.uk/article/the-placebo-problem-big-pharmas-desperate-to-solve14.09.2009 Web

Definitions from Oxford Languages dictionary.com/browse/consciousness Web

Emoto, Masaru. *The Hidden Messages in Water.* Atria Books. Kindle Edition. Originally published in Japanese in 2001 by Sunmark Publishing, Inc., as MizuWaKotae Wo Shitterli Printed

Goodreads.com/quotes/33052-a-mind-is-like-a-parachute-it-doesn-t-work-if Web

Grad, Bernard. "Paranormal Healing and Life Energy." *American Society for Psychical Research Newsletter* 7 (1981) E-book

Dr Lipton, Bruce; Steve Bhaerman. *Spontaneous Evolution*: Our Positive Future (and a Way to Get There from Here. Hay House, Inc. -September 2009 E-book

- Bruce H. Lipton Ph.D. *The Biology of Belief*: Unleashing the Power of Consciousness, Matter, & Miracles Kindle 1st Hay House edition, September 2008

Osho *Insights for a New Way of Living* First eBook Edition: December 2011 Library of Congress Cataloging-in-Publication Data Osho, 1931–1990. Intuition: knowing beyond logic / Osho. —1st ed.

Dr. Taylor, Jill Bolte. *My Stroke of Insight.* Hodder & Stoughton. First published 2009 E-book

The professor and the madman movie, *The Professor and the Madman* is a 2019 biographical drama *film* directed by Farhad Safinia (under the pseudonym P. B. Shemran), from a screenplay by Safinia and Todd Komarnicki based on the 1998 book The Surgeon of Crowthorne (published in the United States as *The Professor and the Madman*) by Simon Winchester.

Masters, Paul Leon. *Ministers/Bachelor's Degree Modules.* 1 vols. Sedona, AZ: University of Sedona Publishing, 2012.

Thomson, Max. *Quantum Physics for Beginners* 16 Aug 2020 Self-published E-book

Wikipedia.org/wiki/Consciousness. Web

Washington crime study shows a 23.3% drop in violent crime trend due to the meditating group. (worldpeacegroup.org/washington_crime_study.html) by Hagelin, Bill. Web

Brucelipton.com/*romp-through-the-quantum-field/* Bruce H. Lipton – Web

livescience.com/49404-*viagra-for-premature-babies*.html, By Dr. Edward Shepherd January 10, 2015 – Web

Jstor.org/stable/27522387, *Effects of Group Practice of the "Transcendental Meditation" Program on Preventing Violent Crime in Washington, D.C.: Results of the National Demonstration Project, June-July 1993* Published By: Springer, June 1999 - Web

Printed in Great Britain
by Amazon